Talking

TO DUCKS

Rediscovering the Joy and
Meaning in Your Life

JAMES A. KITCHENS, Ph.D.

A FIRESIDE BOOK   Published by Simon & Schuster
NEW YORK LONDON TORONTO SYDNEY TOKYO SINGAPORE

FIRESIDE
Rockefeller Center
1230 Avenue of the Americas
New York, New York 10020

Designed by Richard Oriolo

Manufactured in the United States of America

10 9 8 7 6 5 4 3 2 1

Library of Congress Cataloging-in-Publication Data
Kitchens, James A.
   Talking to ducks: rediscovering the joy and meaning in your life / James A. Kitchens.
      p.   cm.
   "A Fireside book."
   Includes bibliographical references and index.
   1. Spiritual life.   2. Joy.   3. Kitchens, James A.   I. Title.
BL624.K574   1994
158'.1—dc20   93-34919
                                                                          CIP

ISBN: 0-671-87082-3

The excerpts from *Seasons That Laugh or Weep* that appear on pages 41 and 43, copyright by Walter J. Burghardt. Published by Paulist Press and reprinted by permission.

Excerpts from "Things Not Solved though Tomorrow Came" from *The Horseshow at Midnight and An Afternoon of Pocket Billiards* by Henry Taylor. Copyright © 1992 by Henry Taylor. Published by Louisiana State University Press and reprinted by permission.

Excerpts from *The Voyage of the Dawn Treader* by C. S. Lewis are published by Lions, an imprint of HarperCollins Publishers Limited, and reprinted by permission.

The poem, "Me—A Question" by Dorothy Dickson Rishel, is reprinted by permission of the author. Dorothy Dickson Rishel (who was eleven years of age when she wrote this poem) is now an ordained United Methodist Minister and has a Ph.D. in clinical psychology.

Excerpts from *The Power of the Powerless* by Christopher de Vinck, copyright © 1988 by Christopher de Vinck, are used by permission of Doubleday, a division of Bantam Doubleday Dell Publishing Group.

Excerpts from *The Song of the Bird* by Anthony de Mello, copyright © 1982 by Anthony de Mello, S.J., are used by permission of Doubleday, a division of Bantam Doubleday Dell Publishing Group.

Excerpts from *Soul Making* by Alan Jones, copyright © 1985 by Alan Jones, used by permission of HarperCollins Publishers.

Excerpts from *The Primal Mind* by Jamake Highwater, copyright © 1981 by Jamake Highwater, are used by permission of HarperCollins Publishers.

continued on page 208

To Rachel, with love

Beloved, we are always in the wrong,
Handling so clumsily our stupid lives,
Suffering too little or too long.
Too careful in our selfish loves:
The decorative manias we obey
Die in grimaces round us every day.
Yet through their tohu-bohu comes a voice
Which utters an absurd command—Rejoice.

—W. H. Auden, *"In Sickness and in Health"*

CONTENTS

Acknowledgments

I wish to thank the hundreds of students, friends, and clients with whom I have shared life over the last twenty years. They have taught me far more than I have ever taught them, and they have contributed to my healing as a person in ways far beyond their awareness or my own.

I have included many of their stories in the pages that follow because I believe that a story conveys truth more efficiently than a lengthy explanation. Every story in these pages is true. If the individual whose story is being shared is designated by both first and last name, the account is true down to the last detail. Each of these persons has read what is said of him or her in these pages and has given permission for his or her story to be included. If only a first name is given, the story is a composite of stories of a number of clients with whom I have worked as a therapist.

I have also included my own story, because I know myself better than I know anyone else.

Preface

"And they lived happily ever after."

So ends the childhood story. The struggle is over, and everybody is safe and happy. We can all breathe easier because the big, bad wolf is destroyed, the witch-mother has been thrown into the oven, and the giant has fallen to his death as Jack chopped the beanstalk down. The danger is past and the victory won. Everything's okay.

These stories, and their adult counterparts, encourage us to divide life into good and bad. We seek the good and dodge the bad. Struggle, conflict, and turmoil are bad. Bad is losing and not getting the things we want. Good, on the other hand, is winning and having all the things we desire. These stories encourage us to believe that joy and peace and happiness are possible only after the struggle is over. Like the hero of an old western, we believe that if we confront the enemy with courage and the will to win, we will inevitably overcome. Right prevails. The conflict ends, and we ride away victorious into the sunset. With each struggle we await the delightful outcome of winning the final victory, getting what we want, and living "happily ever after."

But life doesn't turn out like that at all. As Edna St. Vincent Millay reminds us, "It is not true that life is one thing after another—it's one damn thing over and over."

Life offers no final victory. In fact, life offers no final anything. We describe life as *process*, a word originating from a Latin root that means "to go forward." Process is what happens between the beginning of a journey and the arrival at a destination. But the process of life is not a straight line. Rather, it is a circle and, as such, involves continuous development, change, variety, and growth. To experience life as a process, then, we must advance.

The process does not end so long as life itself does not end. Nor should we want it to, because joy is found as much *during* the journey as in the arrival. Life's constant movement and challenges are the birth-pangs of the soul. The paradox of the soul is that we find joy in *becoming*.

Of course, accomplishment feels good. A job well done gives great satisfaction. But there are equally great joys which we may discover in the process. Once Christopher Robin asked Winnie the Pooh what he liked doing best in the world. Pooh took some time to reflect before answering. Eating honey was high on his list, and he knew that it was a very good thing to do. Yet he realized that "there was a moment just before you begin to eat it which was better than when you were." Pooh somehow knew that the anticipation and the process are preferable to achieving the goal.

I am a teacher, and if I were to answer Christopher Robin's question I would have to say that one of the things I like best is to teach. Actually, there are times when I am so wrapped up in my class that I "get lost." That is, I get so "into" the process that I forget what I am trying to accomplish in the lesson and where I want the lecture to go. I sense a connection with my students. Really, the word *connection* doesn't convey the scope of what is happening to me. Rather, it is as if there were only one mind in the room and we are all part of it. The event of learning unites us, and we are one. I lose myself in this event and sometimes do not know where I am. The paradox is that I feel the most like myself when I am the most lost in this kind of experience.

Everything changes when I begin to check on my performance. When I start to measure my progress toward some preconceived goal, I am no longer immersed in what is occurring. Maybe that is what Yogi Berra meant when he said, "You can't hit and think at the same time." When we *think* about doing something, we begin to evaluate how we are doing. We get involved with the question of how well we are living up to others' expectations. We compare and compete. When I start comparing, I am not lost any longer because I have an external point of reference by which to evaluate myself. But I *lose* myself in a fundamentally different way. I am no longer becoming me. My soul is shriveling up rather than being born.

This book is not about the joy of the final victory. It is not a book that will tell you how to win and therefore feel good about yourself. There is not a word here about how to beat out the competition and get a bigger slice of the pie. This isn't even a book about how to make life more comfortable. It is a book about finding joy in the real world.

The key, however, is not in this book. Rather, it is in the heart of each of us. We possess it already, but we do not know it. We do not have to create it; all that is necessary is that we discover it. This book is, for that reason, like a mirror. It reflects only what is there. As we study the image we see, insight comes. This book probes; it asks questions and encourages us to look within for honest answers. It confronts and cajoles and points the way to growth.

This book is about finding the horses and talking to ducks. Actually, these are two truths about each of us; let me tell you what I mean: once there was a young man who set out on a journey to find a famous religious master who he believed could give him enlightenment. He packed his bags, saddled his horse, and, after saying his goodbyes to his relatives, rode away to find the distinguished teacher. Over mountains, through plains, and across rivers he rode, seeking the great authority who would open his soul.

Weeks later the exhausted young man arrived at a small town where a local monk informed him that the master lived in the hills nearby. The next morning the young man found the old teacher sitting in front of the cave where he lived. Dismounting his horse, the youth asked humbly, "Venerable master, give me enlightenment."

The old man made no response.

Undaunted, the disciple entreated again, "Oh, venerable master, give me enlightenment." There was still no answer. All day long the youth patiently besought the old man to enlighten him. He got no response.

Finally, just at dusk, the young man made his request again, "Venerable master, will you give me enlightenment?"

Looking up at him, the old sage replied, "Why did you not ask me for a horse?"

Surprised, the young man explained, "Because I already have a horse." With that the master arose and went into his cave.

What is true of this young man is true of each of us: We already have the very things we are seeking. That is what D. H. Lawrence meant when he wrote,

> Far back, far back in our dark soul,
> the horse prances. . . .
> The horse, the horse!
> The symbol of surging potency
> and power of movement, of action. . . .

We already have the horse, and that is why this book teaches us to talk to ducks. At least that is what Michael Leunig, an Australian cartoonist, advises us to do in his book *A Common Prayer.* One day he drew a simple picture of a man kneeling in a prayerful posture before a duck. The man in the picture is a peculiar little creature with big eyes and a bigger nose, and no clothes at all. There he is, on his knees before a normal-looking duck with white feathers. It is, Leunig admits, an absurd image. But we must remember that the search for the sublime often has a ridiculous beginning and that nothing is as it appears on the surface.

Kneeling symbolizes humility. An upright stance denotes the qualities of power, stature, control, rationality, worldliness, pride, and ego. We can talk to a duck only from a kneeling position. Kneeling puts us closer to the duck's level and opens us to the absurd possibility of communication with a duck.

The duck, Leunig explains further, represents nature, instinct, feeling, beauty, innocence, the primal, the nonrational, and "the mysterious unsayable." These things, he insists, are all attributes of the inner person, the spirit within. The duck is the symbol of our own inner being. The duck is the human spirit.

The whole picture is the image of our inner exploration, the search for our soul. Leunig's cartoon encourages us to begin the search. And it reminds us that a certain humility and humanness is required. We are called upon to give up our defenses. And we must develop new and more intuitive mechanisms if we are to succeed in this venture of inner discovery.

Further, his cartoon reminds us that inside each of us is an unseen dimension. It is the hidden and, too often, unknown aspect of us. It is our intuitive, spiritual, creative, sentimental, loving, gentle, and natural component. In this book, we call this inner dimension "the soul," but in reality its name is unimportant. What is imperative is that we are aware of it and that it contributes to our being.

In this regard, we are like a tree. Every tree has an unseen part, a part beneath the ground, which I am told is equal in both size and importance to what we see above the ground. For every twig, leaf, and limb that exists above ground, there is an exact counterpart that exists among the roots. Both components are necessary for the life of the tree, and no tree may grow to its fullest potential if either segment is retarded. We, like the tree, must somehow balance both the inner and the outer dimensions, the rational and the intuitive, the material and the ethereal, the worldly and the spiritual. We must find and balance the horses and the ducks within. When both sides of our humanness are in accord, we are able to live more harmoniously with everything around us. As we come to terms with this dimension within, we find a sense of meaning and purpose in life. Though nothing changes out there, everything is different because we are not the same inside.

Finding the horses within and talking to ducks teaches us that there is something *real* at the center of each of us. That mysterious dimension is strong, warm, loving, competent, and wise. We can listen to and trust and follow that part of ourselves. It is our soul, the goal of our spiritual quest. It is the person we genuinely are. And we find in the heart of that faraway person, the real one who lives deep inside us, the solutions to all our problems. And from that source comes the joy that this book is about. It is the joy of the soul.

Godspeed.

JAMES A. KITCHENS
University of North Texas
Denton, Texas

Chapter 1

❖

Joy and the Rediscovery of the Soul

One's actual self may be far from "real," since it may be profoundly alienated from one's deep spiritual identity. To reach one's real self, one must in fact be delivered from that illusory and false self whom we have created. . . . To use common figures of speech, we must "return to ourselves."

—Thomas Merton

❖ *The purpose of life is joy.*
We instinctively know this when we are children. Healthy children are excited, enthusiastic, spontaneous, curious, self-confident, and creative. We play, learn, rest, and live without premeditation or coaxing. Fear, if it appears at all, is rare. Each one of us accepts and loves his or her body and, instead of having to control it and hide it for shame, treats it as a medium through which we express our life and feel our happiness. We enter each new day with expectation and end it exhausted and ready for peaceful sleep. We grow and change each day with neither thought nor effort. We are filled with hope and optimism. Life is joy.

As we grow older, we lose our souls. We learn about failure and disapproval and rejection, and we begin to fear. We risk less, and our natural creativity is swallowed up in our worry about inadequacy. We become careful and controlling as we compare ourselves to others, evaluate and grade ourselves, and compete in order to avoid being perceived as a failure. Caution and suspicion replace trust and openness. We live in order to collect things and achievements, which become badges we wear. We hope to prove to ourselves and to anyone else who might be looking that we are not losers. We forfeit ourselves, and life becomes hard.

Christopher de Vinck, in his book *The Power of the Powerless*, tells a simple but profound story that emphatically illustrates the contrast between the soul of a child and what we too often become along the way:

> One spring afternoon my five-year-old son, David, and I were planting raspberry bushes along the side of the garage. . . . A neighbor joined us for a few moments. . . . David pointed to the ground. . . . "Look Daddy! What's that?" I stopped talking with my neighbor and looked down.
>
> "A beetle," I said.
>
> David was impressed and pleased with the discovery of this fancy, colorful creature. My neighbor lifted his foot and stepped on the insect giving his shoe a twist in the dirt. "That ought to do it," he laughed.
>
> David looked up at me, waiting for an explanation, a reason. . . . That night just before I turned off the light in his bedroom, David whispered, "I liked that beetle, Daddy."
>
> "I did too," I whispered back.

We start our journey like David, curious and accepting and joyfully engaged in every aspect of life. As we travel our path we too often become the neighbor: cynical, untrusting, and fearful. We lose our spontaneous interest in life, and, out of our fear, anger and ignorance, we start to crush the fancy and colorful creatures that we encounter. In the process, we crush ourselves.

This loss is not irrevocable. We are not hopelessly trapped. We can regain the spontaneous curiosity and openness that is characteristic of a child. No matter where we are in life, no matter the muddle we have made or the fix we are in, we can rediscover the joy for which our lives were originally created. The potential that exists within us is as real as the day we were born. The secret is to find our way back to our original selves—our soul.

That is what finding the soul is about. It is about reverting to the joy and fullness and excitement and hope that we had before we learned about the fear of rejection and failure. It is about shucking the false and illusionary self we have created and returning to our true selves, to the joy that comes from fully accepting what we are. It is about returning to our state of being before our soul was murdered. It is about how we rediscover an enthusiasm for living and a purpose for our life. It is about the question, How can life become fun again?

The Journey Forward Is the Journey Back

Today I like my life. I have a settled feeling of satisfaction with who I am. I have confidence and security and a feeling of competence about my life. I have a sense of where I came from that includes the pain and ugliness of my past. I feel comfortable with where my life is going, including the bumpy and unpleasant parts. And I have a peaceful acceptance of where I am today, including the places I do not like and wish were different. I feel optimism and hope and efficacy all rolled up into one.

There are times that I am overwhelmed with joy. A

21

physical and psychological feeling suddenly sweeps over me without any premeditation or preparation on my part. It is like a physical presence that wells up inside me, and for a few seconds or minutes I lose myself. I do nothing to create the feeling. It seems to come of its own will while I am busy doing something else. Walking across a parking lot, pulling weeds from my flower bed, sitting down to a meal, conversing quietly with my wife—there in my heart without warning comes an overwhelming sense of quiet, satisfying joy.

The joy of which I am speaking is not the ecstasy or sudden euphoria that comes from my team winning a game or my getting the promotion, or even from the news that the tumor was benign. These are wonderful and meaningful events, and we all seek them. But the experience I am speaking of is more than a temporary, punctilious occurrence that comes about because of some external circumstance.

The joy to which I am referring is not a denial of problems or a dismissal of the hard spots in life. It is not based on a head-in-the-sand rejection of reality. It does not require that we suspend our rationality and play the part of a grinning idiot. It is not a disavowal of the contradictions of life or of the actuality of events in our lives that are beyond explanation. The joy I describe is a hard-headed realism that squarely faces the inhumane and punishing facts of life but nonetheless arises, because it is a part of my inner being.

I have not always had this feeling. As I look back, I sometimes think that I came into the world scared. I have no recollection of being a healthy, fun-loving child. My earliest memories are of being afraid. I was cautious and timid with my father, who was an undependable alcoholic during my growing-up years. He was big and strong and unpredictable when he was drunk. On the other hand, my mother was a depressed woman who found solace in a rigid religious system and in martyring herself to her brothers and sisters and parents. I saw myself as responsible for making her happy and yet felt impotent to do it. I knew only two absolute methods for gaining her approval: first, I could not grow up to be like my father; and second, I had to be religious.

When my mother's sadness and depression emerged, my heart broke for her. I felt guilty and weak because I could not overcome whatever was hurting her or bring joy to her life. I lived in a state of loneliness and self-deprecation. I felt cowardly and unfit. There was not much happiness in my life during those years.

What I learned as a child I practiced as a young man. In my early adulthood, I felt afraid and disappointed in myself. As a result I was angry much of the time, and the anger was even more dangerous because I did not realize that I was angry. I believed I was less adequate than other people. The reality was that I was an outstanding success. I made top grades in graduate school and received my first of two doctorates when I was only twenty-seven years old. In my twenties I also had unusual success in my profession. My achievements always seemed to be ahead of schedule and came easily. From the outside, everything looked great. My problem was what was inside. I doubted and second-guessed myself, and I felt inferior and somewhat fake. I was not happy, and I wasn't enjoying my life.

I had a powerful internal system to detect other people's expectations and forced myself to live up to their standards. Not only could I not be me, I even lost the capacity to *know* me. I was like a doughnut; the exterior was perceptible, but the center was vacant. So, no matter what I did or achieved, there was no joy, because it wasn't me who was chalking up these victories. It was some other guy that I was trying to be.

At age thirty-two, I received my second doctorate and became a university professor. Things were looking good for me because I was going in the right direction, but I was still carrying extra baggage. Although I was hyperalert to what others expected of me, this time the expectations were not at all clear. I was playing on a field with unknown boundaries and obscure rules. I had to win a game I didn't know how to play. I sank into an abyss of work and alcohol. I worked at a frenzy that was designed to help me win, and again I made what looked to the outsider like positive achievements. But the result inside was the same kind of frustration and emptiness. I used booze to help forget the pain and sense of failure.

Strangely enough, I *was* in the right place. My native temperament and interests were right for being a teacher. I am a gentle and caring person by nature, I like people, I am intellectually curious, and I had what it took to be a professor. People who observed me saw a young man who was doing well and exhibiting all the signs of being happy. I had no apparent reason to be otherwise. I had no right to be anything but happy.

But it did not feel that way inside. In the dark places of my heart, I felt unhappy and dissatisfied. My personal and family life fell apart, and I was divorced by my wife of thirteen years. She moved, taking my son of five and a daughter of one, five hundred miles away.

My parents could not understand what was happening and could not forgive me for the wrongs they perceived me to have committed. I was completely alone. I was trying to do my best to get it right by pleasing people, to win their approval and love. But it didn't work; I was alone, afraid, sad, and angry.

The bottom fell out one summer evening when I was thirty-four. It was Saturday night, and I was sitting alone in my small efficiency apartment. Crowded into that one room was a chair, a single bed, some kitchen equipment, a tiny desk containing some books and a lamp, and a radio. The bedspread was a loud brown and orange that clashed with the orange and brown shag carpet. My children were five hundred miles away, I had managed to make no friends in the town where I had lived for two years, my only diversion from work was more work, and there was no one who knew or cared how much pain there was in my heart. I was alone in the universe.

It was about ten o'clock. Suddenly I began to cry. The tears came in deep sobs that racked my whole body. The sadness filled my chest with an ache that threatened to explode through my throat. I could not sob hard enough. I rose from my chair and fell across my bed face-down. The tears came with a sense of relief as the great sadness and broken-heartedness of my life came rushing forth. I was glad I was crying. It was a letting-go of all the hurt of my entire life.

I don't know how long I cried. Suddenly, I became afraid that I could not stop. I thought, "What if you can't stop these tears and you can't do your work and everybody finds out what a weakling and a fake you really are?" These thoughts overwhelmed me. The tears continued. Now, however, they were not relieving and healing; they were tears of fear.

Finally, I got up and went outside. The night was warm and the stars were bright, and as I concentrated on the sounds of the evening, I managed to stop crying. I lived on the second floor, and I stood on the outside balcony and watched the city about me. I could see cars moving on the street. Half a block away was a convenience store, and as I stood there, I could see the customers coming and going. Other apartment buildings with neatly trimmed hedges and grass were nearby. I tried to make myself focus on anything except my pain.

Slowly, I began to pull myself under control. Then a new thought hit me like a tidal wave destroying everything in its path. "What if I'm not really here," I thought. "I don't know for sure that I'm really here. How can I know that I'm here?" These thoughts kept racing through my brain. I felt both absolute terror and overpowering sadness. It was as if a nice person who had never been alive had died and I was grieving his death.

Again, I have no idea how long I stood there with that sense of vacancy. Finally, I decided that I would put my existence to the test. I walked a block or two toward the university where I taught and took a seat on a bench near some late-night fast-food restaurants and waited for a patron to come out. My plan was simple and foolproof: if another person acknowledged me in some way, I would know that I existed.

I waited. Soon a couple appeared from a convenience store up the street and headed my way. They were holding hands and talking. The young man was carrying a six-pack of beer. They didn't even look my way as they passed. My heart sank. "I knew it," I whispered to myself, "I am not here." Dejected and disappointed, I sat there for an indeterminate amount of time. It was well after midnight, and the street was empty except for the solitary and lost figure sitting on that park bench. I began to cry again.

Some time later, I made the decision to go into the store from which the couple had emerged and try to buy something. If the clerk took my money, I reasoned, it would prove that I did exist. I bought a pack of gum. The clerk's comment when she took my change was among the sweetest words I ever heard: glancing vaguely in my direction she said, "Thank you." I headed back into the night thinking, "Maybe I do exist."

Today I know that the problem was that *I did not exist.* My fear and desperation were not a figment of my imagination. I, as *me,* the genuine essence that I am, did not exist. I was buried under years of garbage and refuse. My life had been a morass of attempts to be someone else, someone whom other people wanted me to be. That night of pain and fear unmistakably dramatized that I did not know me, that I was not being me. And I knew that I had better do something about it.

My journey from there to here has taken twenty years, lots of hard work, and many more tears. I believe that the feelings of overwhelming joy I experience come from the knowledge that I *do* exist and that I am glad I do. The medieval mystic Meister Eckhart had a simple formula for joy. He wrote, "Wisdom is found in doing the next thing you have to do, doing it with your whole heart, and finding delight in it." I had lived with a lack of wisdom, which became a personal crisis for me. The problem was not that I had knowingly chosen to be deliberately foolish but that I had followed in a blind and unthinking way the pattern of those who had gone before me. Their example had become a rut that had shut off options all too often, leaving me trapped. I was feeling the same helplessness and impotence of the child who believed he must make his mother happy but who didn't even know why she was so unhappy. I was the victim of the circumstances, relationships, obligations, and limited competencies.

The Preaccomplishment Me

When I speak of the "soul," I am referring to the authentic self, the real me, my whole person. I do not use the term in a religious context here. The soul is my unique essence, but it is not separate from my body. There is not, as some contemporary theologies would teach us, a battle between body and soul. The flesh is not some dirty prison in which the soul is temporarily incarcerated and from which it longs to be free. I do not, as Plato suggested, lose my soul because I descend into human flesh. Rather, I am separated from my essence as I lose contact with the "me inside me," my actual self. When I live in denial of what I truly am, I lose my soul and, along with it, the joy of life. When I say only what is expected of me, when I sell a product I do not believe in, when I try to teach others what I myself am not committed to, when I act as if I love things or persons that in fact I do not, when I reject things that I want to have as an integral part of me, when I pretend not to feel things that I do in reality feel, when I hate my body, when I fear my sexual self, I lose my soul. And when I lose my soul, I lose my joy.

Wordsworth spoke of what he called "unknown modes of being." That, it seems to me, is the soul. It is the part of us that we can never fully comprehend. It is the mystery of life and of our own being. It is *numen*, or spirit. It is the other presence within us that we can never fully articulate or explain, the part that transcends our physical senses. The soul is our *unknown* mode of being.

Thus, my soul is my whole being, the totality of my personhood. It is my mind, personality, temperament, history, future, body, and potential. It is the genuine part of me, the spontaneous part, the part of me that can be empathetic and compassionate. My soul is my vulnerability, playfulness, intuition, my private and inward me. In short, my soul is the true or authentic me rather than a false or unauthentic self. Soul, for me, points to the unique person who is me, my true self, the qualities and characteristics that are me. It is the preaccomplishment me, the me before I obtained the academic degrees or collected the material symbols of success and achievement. It is the wonderful qualities that I possessed as an infant. It is the helpless and imperfect child who is vulnerable and weak and dependent, who has no bank account or profession or resume. Yet that child is intrinsically valuable, unique, and special.

Let me demonstrate one important way to discover the soul. Galveston, Texas, represents one of the most unhappy aspects of my life. I lived there as a preschooler. My father was a carpenter, and he had moved our family there so he could work in a shipyard. He was in the throes of his alcoholism, and we were poor and undesirable, a small part of the flotsam of life that passed through the world unregarded and unknown. I still carry the pain of this formative period of my life, and it still affects the way I live as an adult. I want to begin to heal the hurt and work with this part of my life. To do so, I can go back in my mind to that time and find the child that I was then. In a sense, I can rewrite my past. The image that I create can be a healing experience.

To do this, I close my eyes, quiet my spirit, and relax my body, and any images that want to appear just come into my mind. In my mind's eye, I can see myself as a child playing on a small stretch of beach near my home in Galveston. The child I see is about three years old, barefooted, and dressed in a pair of yellow shorts and a white T-shirt. On the shirt are the words "Fragile: Handle with Care." The child ambles about, inspecting sea shells. A crab at the water's edge catches his attention, and he bends from the waist, his nose almost touching the water as he curiously studies the crab. He notices a small, reddish rock and picks it up and puts it in his pocket. He looks up to watch a seagull fly silently overhead. Suddenly he is running, splashing water and wet sand up over his body. He throws his body down and rolls about in the deliciously warm sand. Nearby, sitting on a rock, is the child's father. The child strolls over and pulls himself into his father's strong arms. The father is quick to receive the child, hugs him warmly, and kisses his cheek gently. The child, relaxed and secure, rests there in his father's arms as the two of them watch the family dog approach. There is a delighted smile on the child's beautiful face.

As I contemplate the vision I have created, I become aware that I have just beheld my own essence. The child is the paragon of my inner being. To know the characteristics of the child is to be aware of that inner essence, to know my own soul. As I isolate myself from this image, a number of characteristics about the child, and thus about my soul, come to mind: he is comfortable being alone because his aloneness is solitude, not loneliness. He is independent, curious, sensitive, aware of life, and open and inquisitive. He feels comfortable in relationships and accepts love as a deserved gift. These are characteristics of the child and are, therefore, qualities that are intrinsically and eternally mine.

We are not limited to returning to our childhood to discover our soul. We can do the same with our adult selves. For example, not long ago I was in a meeting with a group of faculty members at my university. I related a personal story about myself when I was about twenty-five years old. The story conveyed my deep desire at that age to help people and expressed how I had carried that idealism to my teaching. Before finishing the tale I was aware that my peers were unimpressed with the ideals that my narrative revealed about me. One made a sarcastic remark, and the others laughed. I felt rejected and humiliated but "good naturedly" laughed with them at myself and then fell silent.

On the way home, I could not forget the pain I felt in the meeting. I interpreted my colleagues' behavior as a direct and personal rejection of me. I had to do something to remove that hurt. Ahead was a small park of shade trees and picnic benches, and I turned my car toward the entrance and pulled over. It was quiet, and for that moment I had complete privacy.

Slowly I let my mind return to the young man I was when I was twenty-five. I saw his generous smile and compassionate eyes. I let my mind's eye peer into his heart to see the caring empathy he felt for people around him. I allowed myself to remember in detail his commitment to helping them. I felt again his disappointment that he was so limited in his ability to make the world a better place. I concentrated on everything that I felt my peers despised. I gave myself permission to look at the idealism from every possible perspective and to accept it completely. "What are the labels I would attach to this young man?" I asked myself. I saw these words: *loving, compassionate, empathetic, aware, idealistic, impressionable, caring, faithful,* and *worthy.*

I wrote these terms on the envelope in which I had received the announcement of the meeting. Then I added, "These things are what I am. They are what make me *me* and are among the things that make me valuable. I am these things, and I will in no way deny or reject them. They are my soul, and I love and accept them as the quintessence of me. They are my substance. I love and accept the young man whose soul is revealed in these attributes and reject any other person's rejection of that young man. It is okay for me to be me!" With that I left the park. I noticed that I hummed as I drove home.

What I now know, and what gives me joy and hope and optimism, is that what makes me a valuable and worthwhile person today is no more and no less than what made me valuable and worthwhile when I was a child and a young man. Those are the qualities of the real me, the authentic self that I am. They are the things of which my soul is made. As I become that self, I am truly being me. But I may, if I so choose, deny or reject that self. In his elegant poem *Ode*, Wordsworth wrote of our soul rising like "life's star" from "God who is our home." "Heaven exists" in the soul of the child at infancy like the "trailing clouds of glory" that characterize the universe. Unfortunately, according to Wordsworth, life is the journey from that point toward the loss of our soul: "Shades of the prison-house begin to close / Upon the growing boy." Youth experiences the constriction of the soul, and finally, in Wordsworth's sad words, "At length the Man perceives it die away, / And fade into the light of common day." When I fail for whatever reason to be the me that I am, I enter this "prison-house," and what began as shining stars in the heavens ends up being only the light of the common day. I bury the real me and lose my soul.

Jesus was perhaps the first to suggest that adult well-being was tied in some important way to rediscovering the healthy parts of childhood. He said simply that if we are to enter God's kingdom, we must become a child. Friedrich

31

Nietzsche no doubt had something similar in mind when he said back in the nineteenth century, "In every real [person] a child is hidden that wants to play." Much has been written of late about this inner child, a concept that, it seems to me, has validity and usefulness in self-discovery and emotional healing. I am touched and instructed in much of what I observe in children today, and I have grown in my own self-respect and self-acceptance by memories, both positive and negative, of my own childhood.

I saw a picture of a child in a magazine recently. I think it was a little boy about eight or ten. I identified with this child; he was spontaneously being what he was and showing his soul for all the rest of us to see. He was running as fast as he could. One arm was thrown out in front of him, and the other was extended behind. He was running so fast that his coat was pulled back in the wind. There was an enormous grin of delight and joy on his face.

I was overwhelmed with the picture. In the moments that I studied the picture, I became that child: exuberant, confident, healthy, strong, uncontrolled, excited, happy, thrilled, competent, freely expressing what was in his body. He ran, I believed, not because something was chasing him or because someone had a clock on him or because he was late or because he feared disappointing someone if he didn't run. Rather, he ran because it felt good to run! He ran because he wanted to run, because he could run, because his body said *run,* because he was a runner. He ran because running is what he did. He ran for joy.

Chapter 2

GETTING IT BACK

Be patient with everyone, but above all, with yourself. I mean, do not be disheartened by your imperfections, but always rise up with fresh courage. I am glad you make a fresh beginning daily. There is no better means of attainment to the spiritual life than by continually beginning again, and never thinking that we have done enough. How are we to be patient in dealing with our neighbor's faults if we are impatient in dealing with our own? He who is fretted by his own failings will not correct them. All profitable correction comes from a calm and peaceful mind.

—ST FRANCIS DE SALES

❖ *The purpose of inner healing* is the rediscovery of our soul. And that is not easy. Most of us simply want the pain to go away. We want relief, not recovery. We resist change and want everything to stay the same while, conversely, we hope that all the wrong will quietly and magically disappear.

Most of us are tired of doing things the same old way —at least that is what we say. But we are afraid we can never change, and we believe we will always have the same problems with which we have struggled all our lives. We are sincerely afraid that we will hurt or inconvenience others if we change. We feel stuck, trapped, cornered, entangled in a web that is too big or complicated to straighten out. We begin sentences with the words "I can't ever . . . ," or "I will never be able to . . . ," or "I always . . . ," or "Every time . . . ." And the feeling behind these phrases is that things are going to stay exactly the way they have always been. There's nothing that we can do.

When we come down to it, we find it hard to give up the old patterns and to try new things. Even when we are in pain over the established routines, we resist changing them. We stay stuck and keep on doing things the same old way. The risk is simply too great for us. Our hope is that someone else will change and make it easy on us or that somehow things will turn out differently this time and we will be okay. We look for a miracle and pray for the easy way. It is hard to give up old patterns and habits, even when we know that they are bad for us or that there is a better, more fulfilling way.

But we must be prepared to lose everything as we turn back to the child and discover the joy for which we were created. Recovery is at first as much a ravaging force as it is a healing. It rips away our previous defenses and shatters the structures and foundations we constructed in weakness and ignorance. Nothing of the old self is sacred or inviolate. We must be prepared to surrender the dysfunctional and destructive patterns of thought, behavior, and feelings that have so long served as coping devices in our lives. Many— perhaps most—adult rules and beliefs must undergo change. Some must die. We must learn new scripts as we ready ourselves for a new role in a new play. Like the man in one of Jesus' parables, we must first dispose of some of our precious possessions if we are to purchase the pearl of great price.

People with cancer must change if they have any hope for life. To live they must develop a radically new life-style. Many of the things that they formerly thought were so necessary for personal satisfaction, such as sedentary activities and certain foods, turn out to be unimportant. They replace these activities with fundamentally different endeavors.

Recapturing our souls is not so different from recovering from cancer. We suffer from soul-cancer, a debilitating and lethal dis-ease. Severe changes are necessary for us to rediscover joy. We must remake ourselves in an entirely different image.

Developing the New You

Like a cancer patient, we must change. What and how are we to change? What are the things we must give up and, just as important, what are we to put in their place? The following are some of the life structures that must be demolished if we are to open ourselves up to the joy that is our birthright.

RELAXING OUR GRIP   Most of us live life with clenched fists as we try to control all the variables in our lives. We will accept only a limited set of outcomes in any situation, and we wish to avoid all others. We strain to make reality conform to our desires and, in the process, consume all our energy trying to control things. We must learn to loosen our stranglehold.

The concept of relinquishing control is diametrically opposed to the principles that our competitive society has taught us are necessary for success. We were taught that we must have drive and ambition and learn to fight for what we want. We can never let down our guard, never let the opposition know that we are sweating. The good life is based on knowing and following these and similar principles.

Not so, say the new standards. More is available to us

than our own redoubled efforts. The simple truth is that the growth principles that govern human life are no less than those that regulate nature's world. That is, a human grows and fulfills the inner potential in the same way that, say, an acorn becomes an oak tree. Within that small seed is all the information (notice even that the word *information* encompasses "formation from within") necessary for the entire life span of the oak. Every leaf, twig, and branch of its hundred-year life is preprogrammed in the genetic code within the acorn. All that is necessary is that the acorn be placed in a reasonably hospitable environment, and what is within externalizes in the reality of the tree.

This inner drive toward growth is precisely what Dylan Thomas had in mind in his poem, "The Force That Through the Green Fuse Drives the Flower," He wrote:

> The force that through the green
>   fuse drives the flower
> Drives my green age. . . .
> The force that drives the water
>   through the rocks
> Drives my red blood.

Any growth is a spiritual experience. That is, the growth of both tree and human is something that happens to us, not something that we do or control with either our mind or our senses. We surrender to it; we do not cause it to happen.

What we are talking about here is real, *not* simply metaphor. The reality is seen clearly in the process of breathing. Nothing is more necessary for life, more personal, or, it would seem, more under our control. Surely breathing is something we do, not something that happens to us. But under careful scrutiny, we observe that we do not make ourselves breathe. When we inhale, we lower our diaphragm and raise our rib cage. These acts increase the size of our thoracic cavity, the hollow opening into which our lungs extend like two balloons. The increased size of the thoracic cavity reduces the inner pressure so that it is less than the pressure outside our body, which pushes air into our lungs. When we exhale, we simply reverse the whole process.

What all this means is that it is not we who control our breathing but the atmosphere that pushes life into us. We do no more than open ourselves up, and the universe does the rest. We cooperate through slight physical reactions and the heavens push and pull the air in and out of our lungs. This process, spiritual and mysterious, begins the moment we are born and continues every moment of our lives until our death. It is a process that we do not control; we merely surrender to it, and thereby our life is made possible.

I have always found it difficult to relinquish control. I am not a trusting person, and my fear of life had molded me into someone who made elaborate preparations for every activity or event. Nothing was left to chance for fear that something unexpected might occur and do me in. I used immense energy to control every jot and tittle of what was going on around me. The turning point in this regard for me came one summer about ten years ago. I had been invited to attend a retreat sponsored by the Episcopal Diocese of Dallas. It was a weekend session beginning on Friday afternoon and ending at noon on Sunday. The retreat center was nestled in a small valley dotted with live oaks, cedar elms, and small post oaks. The grounds were covered with summer's wildflowers and neatly trimmed lawns. Episcopal lay persons and priests presented sessions that were exciting and informative. Interspersed between lectures were skits and short exercises in which we were invited to answer specific questions about ourselves and explore personal introspection. I was deeply moved by it all.

At the end of the final session, the retreat master asked an interesting and challenging question. "How," he asked, "can we take what has occurred here in this place home with us and back into the business world from which we came?" How, he was asking, can principles we learn and resolutions we make in the quiet atmosphere of a retreat center accommodate the "real world"? He also had an answer for us: "Here is a challenge for you," he said. "Each day for the next month give your heart, mind, and soul to God. Just do it for that day and no more. Say to God, 'Today I give you my heart, mind, and soul.' Do it only once a day, and then forget about it. See what happens to you over those thirty days."

I did it. I just said those words each day. I really meant them, even though I did not really know what they meant. What it accomplished for me was that I learned how to "let go." The day became different for me. I was no longer in control. I did not have to make things happen. I could relax and go with the flow. I found my energy level increased. I felt, strangely, in greater control of myself, somehow more responsible and of infinitely greater worth. My whole outlook on life became different. I was quieter within and more calm without.

I have continued this practice ever since. Every day, with very few exceptions, I offer my life to the Great Spirit for that day. I think through the things I must do that day, the people I will meet, the classes I will teach, the fears and uncertainties I will experience, and I offer it all to God. And I take whatever comes. I judge no outcome as unworthy. For me, there are no "mistakes" or "failures." Every thing, every experience, every person is there for a purpose. Nothing is random, and nothing is out of place. I am exactly where I am supposed to be.

RECOGNIZING THE PROCESS We must come to know that life is process. The journey is more important than the destination. How we travel, what we do along the way, is a thousand times more significant than the goal we achieve. The trip is much more important than the arrival itself.

Somehow we lose sight of this as adults and place all our emphasis on the goal. We spend life anticipating things, good and bad, most of which never happen. And tragically, when we do reach a goal, we are so focused on new goals that we do not stop to enjoy what we have accomplished. I call it *hurdling*. Life is like a series of hurdles to be jumped. As soon as I clear this one, my focus is already on the next one. Life is lived as if we were running to jump the next hurdle.

It turns out that joy is a way of proceeding, not a goal toward which we travel. What this means is that we should enjoy the process because the destination is not what it is all about. Children instinctively realize this. As adults we think that if we are behind, or if others are ahead of us, something must be wrong with us—"They are better, so I have to catch them." Children often arrive late because they stop to observe things along the way.

PUTTING MATERIAL THINGS WHERE THEY BELONG   We must come to know that some things matter more than other things, and we have to determine which are which. We must find higher meaning for ourselves other than through material things. A man said to me recently, "Money gives you freedom." "I disagree," I gently responded. His eyes widened in surprise. "What I mean is that you can travel and buy what you want when you want it," he explained. Again he was convinced that I would now agree. "Not so," I remonstrated. "You are a rich man, are you not?" He nodded in agreement. "And you travel, do you not?" He nodded. Only the day before he had returned with his wife from a week in the Colorado Rockies. "Well," I continued, "Are you free?" He reflected for a moment, thinking about the antidepressant he took each morning and the sleeping pill he took each evening. He remembered his earlier comments about how he hated his job, felt like a fake, and could not change because it would "disappoint" too many people. Moreover, he still owed a lot of money that he had to pay back. "No," he admitted, "I am trapped. I am anything but free."

I felt challenged by his statements and I went home and wrote what I *did* believe could give us freedom. Here is my list:

MY FREEDOM CREED

I am truly free if I can

> *say* what I think rather than what I am supposed to say or what others want me to say;
>
> *ask* for what I want and need instead of what is acceptable to ask for;
>
> *take* risks instead of trying to protect myself and play it safe;
>
> *feel* what I really feel rather than what I ought to feel;
>
> *know* my dreams and follow them rather than do with my life what others expect me to do;
>
> *experience* my body and enjoy it;
>
> *see* and *hear* what is here rather than what I want to be here or what is supposed to be here;
>
> *discover* my sexual values and express them rather than those others set for me;
>
> *trust* that my own inner qualities are my greatest resource for personal growth and change; and
>
> *believe* that I am a Wonderful Person.

Life is more than material success. Mother Teresa put it well in *Words to Love by*. . . . She said simply, "I think people are so preoccupied with material difficulties. In the industrial world where people are supposed to have so much, I find that many people, while dressed up, are really, really poor."

FIND OURSELVES AND OTHERS IN COMMUNITY Being with people, not being in competition with them, is what gives life its spice and excitement. Children know this. They are naturally cooperative and seek others to play with. They do not at first keep score; that is something they have to learn to do. But they do know how to go beyond themselves. Father Walter Burghardt, a Jesuit priest, says it well in his book *Seasons That Laugh or Weep*: "The paradox is, the only way I can get my act together is not in isolation but in relation. I become myself to the extent that I go out of myself. I find my life in the measure that I am ready to risk it. When I can say, to a single person or to an acre of God's world, 'Your life is my life,' then I will begin to come alive."

Finding intimacy in this age of loneliness and anxiety is not easy, but it is essential. Being close to people and feeling that we are significant to them is a necessary ingredient for healthy living. Yet many of us have a hard time finding people with whom we can have this kind of experience. We want closeness and community, or so we say, and we try hard to do the things that we believe will bring genuine intimacy. The result is that too often we end up feeling disconnected and isolated. Sometimes we feel completely alone. Longing for intimacy and closeness, we live crowded together but apart and separated.

Erica Jong, a novelist who many years ago advocated what she called the "zipless fuck," has reached a new awareness. Writing in the May, 1989, issue of *Ms. Magazine*, she says:

> Our society has had a decade and a half of experimentation with random sexual freedom. We have discovered that it is neither so very sexy nor so very free. My generation is disillusioned with sex as a social panacea. We look longingly at the marriages of our parents and grandparents and wonder how on earth they managed to stay best friends for so long—or even worst friends for so long. But at least they had someone to read the newspaper with. Alone in our single-parent families,

still searching for the one great love, we begin to smell a rat. We begin to realize that life consists of little moments of compromise, of joy, of embracing the primal flux. . . . There is finally no substitute for love, for spiritual sharing, for commitment, for cherishing each other.

PLAYING   We must learn that play is more important than work. Most of us work because we are afraid, not because we love what we do. We have to work, or else we lose out—or so we think. We must be constantly vigilant lest others take advantage of us, pull ahead of us, and end up getting our part. Work becomes a rut. The emphasis is on productivity; and even for white-collar professionals, work becomes an impersonal assembly line in which the goal is as much money in as few hours as possible. We work in order to consume. It all degenerates into a dehumanized life-style, a house we cannot pay for in a neighborhood we do not like, which contains people we do not know and who do not know us. In the introduction to his book of poetry entitled *Laughing Down Lonely Canyons*, James Kavanough says: "Ultimately we endure a marriage grown silent, work at a job we can barely tolerate, and ignore our personal feelings until we no longer really know what we want. To survive, we retreat into a prison of our own making. We exist, perform, even achieve an unsatisfying success, dismissing yearnings for intimacy and change as distant impossibilities. We accept life as a burden to be endured with no time to let go. . . ."

What we have plenty of is ambition; what we are short on is a calling. We are impoverished by the loss of the sense of vocation. Kids intuitively know about calling and vocation. Their dreams and visions reveal their idealism. That is the stuff of which high school yearbooks are made. But we have lost our dream. It is drowned in the backwaters of reality, buried under a burden of debt and loss, and hidden from sight in our resentment and fear of failure. And where does that leave us in life? What will we be at age sixty-five? Will we look back on our living years as satisfying and fulfilling? What does our heart say about what our life is about? In Seasons That Laugh and Weep, Walter Burghardt asks, is our work no more than "the drain down which [we are] pouring [our] life"?

We must be careful lest our work mentality creep into our playing. The philosophy that we have to "play hard" can overtake and overwhelm us. Our play can become work. David L. Miller, in his book Gods and Games, reminds us that we can get so involved with playing that our play and reality become one. When this occurs, we are playing well. On the other hand, we can play so poorly that we begin to think our play is work. It is, Miller says—and that's too bad.

In a "Calvin and Hobbs" cartoon, Calvin is unhappy that he is not having enough fun. "It's Sunday," he exclaims with arms extended in frustration. "I've just got a few precious hours left before I have to go to school tomorrow." Hobbs looks on with a perplexed look on his face. "Between now and bedtime I have to squeeze all the fun possible out of every minute. I don't want to waste a second," continues Calvin. "Each moment I should be able to say, 'I'm having the time of my life right now'!" Again with arms thrown wide in exasperation, Calvin says, "But here I am, and I'm not having the time of my life! Valuable minutes are disappearing forever, even as we speak! We got to have more fun!" Hobbs is attentive and sympathetic. "C'mon!" Calvin screams and away they run. "I didn't realize fun was so much work," Hobbs says as they race along. Calvin responds, "Sure! When you're serious about having fun, it's not much fun at all!"

The secret is that play is necessary. For some of us work can be play. But if we can't let our work be play, let us find ways to have fun that aren't work-related. The rule is: let work be play, if you can; if you can't, let play be play. If we can't do what we love, our challenge becomes somehow to love what we do.

GETTING REALLY REAL We must come to know that reality is more than what our physical senses tell us it is. Indeed, what we know in our mind may be more real than what our eyes see and our ears hear. Lame Deer, the famous Sioux shaman, once said, "It is what you see when your eyes are closed that counts."

I once heard Suzanne Hales, a psychotherapist friend of mine and mother of two young daughters, tell a story about her youngest child. Her family was at a Little League baseball game one afternoon, and Emily, aged five, became bored with the festivities. She found a boy about her age and led him into an opening behind the bleachers. "Let's play ball, Billy," she invited her friend. Billy was excited and ready. "Pitch it here," she yelled and waved her imaginary bat through the air. He pitched the make-believe ball through the air toward her. She waited, then swung her bat with a mighty thrust. Away went the ball, high into the sky. "Home run," she shouted as she clapped her hands and ran the bases that neither of them had established. Back went Billy, running with his hands up and his eyes on the ball. "Caught it," he screamed as he leaped high into the air. "Baseball's great," Emily shouted as the two children fell laughing in each other's arms.

What we realize in this tale is that the game going on behind the bleachers was no less real than the game on the field. For Emily and her friend, their ball and bat and bases were just as authentic as the chalked lines and neat uniforms of the most professional team in the country. And they didn't even have to keep score. Emily's home run was in no way negated by the great catch that Billy made.

GET A HORSE I recently attended a workshop presented to a group of counselors by Greg Stanley in which he offered several recommendations on how to avoid burnout. Prior to his talk, he passed out a list of suggestions and, among them, I was surprised to see the words "get a horse." I looked around the room but saw mostly urban types who did not seem the kind of people who would enjoy horseback riding, not to mention mucking out stalls. I wondered what Dr. Stanley really meant.

When he reached that part of his presentation, he explained that this was his way of proposing that we discover and practice something that is special to us and that belongs exclusively to us. His horse filled that function for him. He urged us to find something in which we can get caught up and lose ourselves, something in which we can become totally immersed. When we get involved in that activity, we forget about everything else.

I believe that Dr. Stanley's advice was not only correct but also imperative. We all need something that is important to us, something in which we have a stake, something to which we give ourselves and in which we find purpose.

Our "horse" may be a real horse or a hobby or a cause or even our faith and spirituality. For some it may be working in the yard, and for others it may be a voluntary service. Whatever it is, we do it because it is ours and we enjoy it. It is not something we do because others expect us to do it or because we have to do it. It is voluntary and fun, and it is important for no other reason than that we like it.

To engage freely and wholeheartedly in an activity *because* we want to, and only because we want to, boosts our opinion of ourselves. That may be the real reason that these diversions are good for our mental health; they increase our sense of self-worth.

An important question that we do not ask enough is "What am I worth?" Let us consider that question. What are we *really* worth? "Each of us should carry two rocks in his pocket," the Rabbi said. "On one we should write the inscription 'I am the dust of the earth.' And on the other we should write, 'For me the universe was created.' "

Each one of us is a mixture of two all-embracing truths: we are nothing more than anyone else. Indeed, we are no more than any other of God's creatures in this world. And, conversely, we are the most precious objects in creation. Each person is a unique variation in the universe; no two people are alike. And, paradoxically, all persons are rooted in a common life.

What do you think you are worth? Be careful that you do not fall prey to the "doing" syndrome, a disease common in our world today. If you answer the question of personal worth with a list of roles you play and your competencies in all that you do, you are not thinking at the level that is most beneficial for you. Think about what you *are*, not what you *do*. Answer the question of worth with attributes and inner qualities rather than with accomplishments or credentials. The answer to the question "What are you worth?" is the same as the answer to the question "Who are you?"

"Get a life" is a commonly heard phrase today. As used by most people, this term may mean something negative. But it is still a good idea. Find your own interests that guide your experience in a fashion that gives you meaning and purpose. Discover and practice something beyond your work world that is a genuine expression of yourself. Do it only because it brings you joy.

REARRANGED THINKING PATTERNS
Helen Keller said, "Keep your face to the sunshine and you cannot see your shadow." Most of us are too unaware of how much control we have over what our minds "see" and the impact that what we see has on how we live. What we put in our minds determines what comes out of ourselves. What we think and what we think about is important because our thoughts have enormous impact on what happens in our lives as well as on what is going on in our bodies.

The world's great thinkers from all ages have understood the importance of what we now call "self-talk." These interior conversations are among the most powerful forces that shape our lives. Consider the wisdom in the following statements:

We become what we think about all day long.
—RALPH WALDO EMERSON

There was a child went forth each day
And everything he saw that day, he became.
—WALT WHITMAN

As a man thinks in his heart, so is he.
—JESUS

Science today confirms what religion has intuitively known from time immemorial, that faith, love, and hope can work miracles of healing and restoration.
—JOSEPH H. KRIMSKY

I saw that all things I feared, and which feared me, had nothing good or bad in them save insofar as the mind was affected by them.
—BARUCH SPINOZA

There is nothing good or bad in itself, but thinking makes it so.
—WILLIAM SHAKESPEARE

People are about as happy as they make up their minds to be.
—ABRAHAM LINCOLN

Change your thoughts and you change your world.
—NORMAN VINCENT PEALE

People and things do not upset us, rather we upset ourselves by believing that they can upset us.
—ALBERT ELLIS

Every good thought you think is contributing its share to the ultimate result of your life.
—GRENVILLE KLEISER

Anything that offers hope has the potential to heal, including thoughts, suggestions, symbols and placebos.
—BERNIE S. SIEGEL

When I was a fourth-grader, Mrs. Hurst, the stunning redhead who was my teacher, wrote the following poem on the blackboard. I loved and believed everything she said because she was so beautiful. So I memorized the poem that day and have many times over the years tried to use its wisdom to guide my life.

> Sow a thought,
>> Reap a behavior.
> Sow a behavior,
>> Reap a habit.
> Sow a habit,
>> Reap a character.

Since our thoughts are so powerful, we should consider carefully how to make them what we want them to be. The following three suggestions will help.

1. We can become aware of negative self-statements. These statements usually begin with something like "I'll never be able to get this right . . ." or "My mate [or boss or co-workers or children] will never understand. . . ." We gain greater control over our thoughts by the simple act of identifying the negative images and ideas we put in our heads.

Buddha taught that the mind is like a monkey. That is, it will wildly and carelessly climb whatever tree it chooses and will jump randomly from one tree to another of its own accord until we train it to cling to the tree we wish. Identifying the negative is the first step in training our minds.

2. We can create positive images. We must, of course, be realistic, but we can see ourselves doing what we want to do. If we wish to change a habit, we can imagine ourselves living life without that habit. If there is a significant problem area we wish to focus on and improve, we can write down a single sentence that describes it. Then we can convert that sentence to one that is positive and self-affirming. We then memorize that sentence and repeat it to ourselves when we are reminded of the problem area.

For example, consider a woman who is withdrawn and has a fear of speaking up in a group. If this person wants to work on that problem, she may write down the sentence "I am shy, and I am afraid to speak in a group." This sentence focuses directly on the problem in a concrete way. Striking out that sentence, she could write in its place, "My ideas are good and I may say them to others, if I choose." Or, "If I choose to, I can tell others what I think." Or, "My voice is loud and my words are good and I may shout them from the rooftop, if I please!"

3. David Burns, in *Feeling Good,* an excellent book on the relationship of patterns of thought and depression, says simply, "You feel what you think." He is saying that there are consequences of thought, just as there are consequences of action. We get what we focus on, or, as Wayne Dyer puts it in *You'll See It When You Believe It,* "What you focus on expands."

Consider the following scenario for a moment. Suppose you want recognition for your work. You try hard to do a good job, and you want people around you to be aware of how well you are doing. What you concentrate on, however, is that no one seems to notice you and that other people get all the rewards for excellent work. At first you try to ignore this idea and just work harder. But all the time your eyes are glued on others, observing whether or not they are noticing. You begin to believe there is some kind of favoritism going on, and you quickly become convinced that no one will notice your good work. So with a what-the-hell attitude, you slack off. Why try? After all, no one notices or cares about you.

Obviously, you will not get the recognition you deserve if this becomes your thought pattern. Think about what expands if you focus on the work rather than on the others and their lack of recognition. Or think about what will happen if you focus on your own personal abilities or your value as a person.

Seek growth and abundance. What do you think will happen if these become your patterns of thought? If you are about to enter a potentially tough meeting and all you think about is how hard everybody is going to be on you and how much rejection you are going to meet, what do you think that will do to your confidence? But if you focus on your competence, your preparation, your experience, your sincerity, or even your well-being regardless of how they respond, what expands? How would your life change if you let your mind center on what you are on the inside and what you need for life rather than on what other people have or even on what is missing from your life?

LOVING WHAT WE ARE Finally, we must come to know that we can be only what we are, and that is exactly what God intends us to be. There is an old Jewish story told by Rabbi Herman E. Schaalman and cited in the July/August 1992, issue of *Alive Now!* that beautifully illustrates this point. Once, in a small town, a group of people decided to put together a band to play at weddings and at special occasions such as holidays and when important people came to visit. Anyone who wanted to could be a part of the band. Unfortunately, in that town there lived a fellow named Shlemiel. He was a simple sort of fellow, the kind of person who tries hard to do right but always seems to end up doing wrong. When he played the trumpet, it sounded like somebody was doing something terrible to an elephant.

When he played the violin, dogs howled for miles around. Finally, not wanting to tell him he couldn't be in the band, the people let him play the drum. They figured he couldn't do much harm with the drum—little did they know.

They began playing and for a while Shlemiel kept time with their music. But soon he got excited. And as he became more excited, he beat his drum louder and louder, and less and less in time with the beat of everybody else who was playing. Soon he was playing to his own rhythm altogether, which completely wrecked the tune. They tried again and again to correct the problem, but they never could.

One day they were to play for the visit of the most famous rabbi in the country, Israel ben Eliezer. Wanting everything to be perfect for so celebrated a guest, they told Shlemiel, "Just pretend to play the drum, but do not hit the drum with the stick." Shlemiel agreed to try.

The distinguished visitor arrived on the appointed day, and the band took the stage. There in the crowd sat the important rabbi. The band began to play.

At first Shlemiel did as he was instructed. He only pretended to hit the drum. Then he began to get excited. After all, the famous rabbi was right there before him. Little by little he began to hit the drum. Then he became louder and louder, and less and less in time with everyone else. The band finally had to stop.

Embarrassed, they took Shlemiel by the neck and dragged him to the rabbi to apologize. Before they could speak, Rabbi Israel ben Eliezer said, "Your music was gorgeous. So beautiful, in fact, that I was transported. The heavens opened and there sitting around the throne of God were musicians—a blissful band playing the most rapturous music I have ever heard. What I noted was that only your drummer was in time with that heavenly band."

There may be significant consequences when we make the decision to honor the person we are. Consider Salman Rushdie, the author of *The Satanic Verses*. Because of a perceived insult to the Muslim religion, Iran's Ayatollah Khomeini offered a million-dollar reward for his death, and Rushdie was forced into hiding for his life. Three years later, in December 1991, he made his first public appearance at Columbia University in New York where he made a speech after which he was whisked back into hiding. Among the comments he made on that day was the following:

> I have learned the hard way that when you permit anyone else's description of reality to supplant your own—and such descriptions have been raining down on me, from security advisers, governments, journalists, archbishops, friends, enemies, mullahs—then you might as well be dead. Obviously, a rigid, blinkered, absolutist worldview is the easiest to keep hold of, whereas the fluid, uncertain, metamorphic picture I've always carried about is rather more vulnerable. Yet I must cling with all my might to my own soul; must hold on to its mischievous, iconoclastic, out-of-step-clown instincts, no matter how great the storm. And if it plunges me into contradiction and paradox, so be it; I've lived in that messy ocean all my life. I've fished in it for my art. This turbulent sea was the sea outside my bedroom window in Bombay. It is the sea by which I was born, and which I carry within me wherever I go.

We must all cling in our own way to our own soul.

I sum up my thoughts on the subject with the following poem:

Me,
I am me,
I am only me,
No one else can be me,
I cannot be everything or everyone,
But I can be what I am and I can do what I can.
And because I cannot do everything or be everyone else,
I will do the best I can and I will be the best I can every day.
I will be me.

Changing into the New You

Morton Kelsey, in the *Other Side of Silence,* reminds us that "the lives of most persons are like jewelry stores where some trickster has mixed up the price tags. The diamonds are priced at next to nothing and some worthless baubles at thousands of dollars. Unless we stop business as usual and take stock, we are likely to end up in bankruptcy."

Each of us has been through *formation.* Like clay in the hands of the potter, we have been shaped by forces around us. Most of the time we are unaware of what these forces are and what effect they are having on us. We simply took our form psychologically, spiritually, emotionally, intellectually, and sometimes even physically from the pressures that were placed upon us.

Too often the forces were dysfunctional, and their influence upon us produced unhealthy and unhappy results. We have been deceived. Our fine jewels have been given away, and we have paid too dear a price for the cheap imitations of life. We have unthinkingly *conformed* to the life forces surrounding us. What we need is *transformation.* That is, we need to change our formation. More is required than mere *reformation.* To reform something is simply to rearrange the elements that are already there. What is needed is to overcome or transcend the form. To do so we have to go outside our comfort zone and break old patterns and try new things.

A friend of mine once wrote to me, "I am the main motivating force in my life. Day by day, I initiate the changes that free my emotions and enable my personality to unfold." Too many times we keep on doing the same old things that have repressed our feelings and squelched our personalities. We have simply continued the same actions and obtained the same results. There is an old saying: "If you keep on doing the things you've always done, you keep on getting the things you always got."

Ask yourself the following five questions, and as you do, think of little things as well as big things in your life and in your relationships that you wish to change. Remember, however, that you must be honest and try to look beneath the surface thoughts and explanations that we have always used in these areas. We are concerned in these questions with discovering specifically *what we need to change* (or where we wish to be transformed) and *what it is that holds us* in the old patterns.

1. Think of the saying "To have abundance, we must be doing what we love and loving what we do." Then ask yourself, How does this statement apply to my life? In what ways am I doing what I love? In what ways am I not?

2. What would I be doing differently if I were doing what I love?

3. Considering what I have just written, here are three things *about me* that I wish I could change:

   1.

   2.

   3.

Here are three things *about me* that keep me from changing (or three things I continue to do, think, or feel that bottle me up and keep me stuck):

1.

2.

3.

4. When I am really honest with myself, here is what I fear will happen if I change:

There is a curious thing about making changes like those described in this chapter. The paradox is that everything changes and at the same time everything stays the same. Oriental philosophy incorporates this view in its ancient wisdom on the subject. For example,

Before enlightenment
   chopping wood
   carrying water
After enlightenment
   chopping wood
   carrying water

It is a strange experience to find out that when we change at the level we are talking about, everything is different and yet nothing is different. We live in the same house, look more-or-less the same, and do the same things.

Yet inside, where it counts, nothing is the same. Life goes on pretty much as usual, but our experience of it is radically different. We chop wood and carry water, as always. The difference is that the treasure, which has been there all along, is now perceived. That is joy.

❖

$\mathscr{T}$HE
THREE LEVELS
OF JOY

Circumstances do not make you, they reveal you.

—WAYNE DYER

❖ When I was thirteen, two things occurred that changed my life forever. First, my family moved from Biloxi, Mississippi, to a rural area in south Louisiana. Second, my father developed a disabling and painful form of arthritis that hospitalized and incapacitated him for nearly a year. During this time we lived on the generous gifts of food and money that our rural community gave to us, and, even more significantly for me, my father dried out. He used the onset of the arthritis as a time of reflection and prioritizing in which he developed a stout faith that helped him change his life. He conquered his alcoholism and redirected his life.

It was during these years of early adolescence that I received, for the first time in my life, a taste of joy. My father turned his attention toward me in an effort to make up for lost time. We didn't play together. What we did was work together. He let me become his helper in his carpentry, and he became involved in the farm projects that interested me.

For my part, I loved being with him. He was strong and funny and wise. I felt his love. The experience of being with him stirred, for the first time in my life, feelings of worth and value in my thirteen-year-old soul. He listened and responded with caring advice to my adolescent problems. He gave me a nickname, Buddy, which was a source of immense pride for me because it came, as I saw it, from a bond of affection.

My projects involved farm animals and crops, and consequently I developed a deep love for nature. So formative were those experiences that when I think of joy, my first association is of a scene from those years. Joy to me is a fertile strawberry field. Neat rows of small, dark green bushes line the ground from fence to fence. Round leaves the size of silver dollars cover each plant, and white blooms that will quickly become green fruit and then ripen into large red berries abundantly decorate the whole field. It is February, and the early morning air is still crisp. I can practically smell the pungent, somewhat acidic scent of pine straw, which neatly covers the rows and nestles snugly against the plants.

Across the fence from the field is a rolling pasture of sweet, white Dutch clover turning green in the early spring warmth. A bay horse and three or four jersey cows are peacefully grazing in the grass, which reaches nearly to their knees. Two calves lie in the shade of a small red oak, only their heads showing above the stems of succulent grass. Farther in the distance, tall pines sway gracefully in the wind. Two cardinals, a male and female, sit on the top wire of the fence while several blackbirds chirp happily in the wax myrtle bushes that line the fencerow.

Near the pines, a small pond shimmers among cattails and willow trees. Two white egrets stand knee-deep in the water waiting for an unsuspecting minnow to swim by. The sky is blue with a few wisps of white floating clouds. I am young, filled with optimism and hope, and in love with life. Life seems abundant and full. In my heart is peace and serenity and satisfaction and hope. School is tolerable because I love to learn. I am healthy, my body is strong, and my father loves me.

If we try to understand joy by analyzing this image that inspired my joy, we find it difficult. It is easier to describe joyful things than to explain what joy is. Even the dictionary doesn't help much. It says simply that joy is "a very glad feeling, happiness, great pleasure, delight." In defining joy we often fall back on stiff and exhausted clichés. Joy is satisfaction, peace, serenity. It is a keenly felt, exuberant, often demonstrative happiness. One feels joy when life is going well and we are healthy and strong. Joy is a feeling of great satisfaction. These descriptions, while correct in essence, are not very satisfying to me.

It is also difficult to define joy comprehensively because joy is not limited to a single dimension. There are at least three levels of joy that differ in both source and intensity. Each is important in its own right.

Contingent Joy

Contingent joy is the kind of joy that is dependent on the specific external circumstances of a person's life. It is joy that emerges from a situation. This joy comes on the basis of what is "happening" and may, therefore, be called happiness. Happiness comes from an Old English word, *happ,* which means suitable or convenient. Thus, *happ* is associated with luck or good fortune. If I have good luck, my circumstances are positive and I am happy. For example, I am happy if I get the promotion, if I win the game, if I am elected to the office, if my child performs well in the piano recital, if the picnic is a success, or if I win the prize. On the other hand, if I am hapless, my luck is bad, I don't get what I want, and I am not happy.

Joy at this level—or happiness, as it should be properly called—may be extreme, even overpowering. We can observe intense happiness watching the winning team and their fans at the Super Bowl or World Series or some other sporting event. When external events turn out the way we want them to, we become happy and excited. The more important we consider the event to be, the greater the happiness we experience. We can be overwhelmed with contingent joy.

Twenty-four-year-old Hassiba Boulmerka knows this kind of joy. Her experience, as reported in the August 3, 1992, issue of *Sports Illustrated,* demonstrates how overwhelming contingent joy can be. A fifteen-hundred-meter runner from Algeria, she has had to withstand enormous social and religious pressure to continue her racing career. Doctrinaire and powerful fundamentalist imams in her country pronounced a *kofer,* or denunciation of her as "un-Muslim," for "running with naked legs in front of thousands of men." For years, as she ran on Algerian roads, men had spat or thrown stones at her to convey the contempt they had for her. The country was divided over the very idea of female athletes, and the dispute reached to the highest levels of the military and the government.

In Tokyo in the summer of 1991, this gallant young woman who had strained the very social fabric of her society won the world championship in the fifteen-hundred-meter race. Running in Algerian green, she held well back in the pack until the last lap. She clawed her way clear and, in the homestretch, labored to hold on. No Algerian woman had ever won a world championship. On her narrow shoulders balanced much more than personal pride. Behind her was Tatyana Samolenko Dorovskikh of the USSR, the Olympic three-thousand-meter champion famous for her great strength at the end of the race. Boulmerka told herself that she had been strong all season and she would be strong now. Dorovskikh could not close the gap, and Boulmerka won by three meters. As she passed the finish line she screamed, seizing her hair with both hands. She continued to scream, mouth thrown open, arms extended to the heavens as if her passion were so great that it threatened to explode her heart. "I screamed for joy and for shock," she explained later. "I was screaming for Algeria's pride and Algeria's history, and still more. I screamed finally for every Algerian woman, every Arabic woman."

This level of joy comes and goes with whatever is happening in our environment. It is extrinsic because it arises from the outside and, therefore, is not a quality that comes from within. We are powerless over this kind of joy although we try hard to control it. When the circumstances change in one direction, joy comes. When fortune reverses, this level of joy leaves.

Contingent joy is consumer happiness. It succumbs to the wooing of the manufacturing and advertising world that tells us that if we can consume a specific object, happiness and satisfaction and joy will be ours. To own a certain make of car, to wear a specific brand of jeans, or to drink a precise variety of beer will make all our dreams come true and let us live happily ever after. That is the promise, but of course it doesn't work out that way. Circumstantial joy is temporary.

Unfortunately we spend most of our time and energy seeking contingent joy. We think, "If only this or that would happen, then I could be happy." Or, "If I can only accomplish so and so, I will be happy." Contingent thinking is like eating soup with a fork—we can never get enough. As soon as we accomplish what we think will make us happy, our eyes turn to another contingency, and we think, "Now, if only that will happen, then I will really be happy." Contingent thinking creates a constant tension that pushes us to a life of perpetual incompleteness and unhappiness.

There is nothing wrong with wanting contingent joy in our lives. We all seek good things for ourselves and for those we love. Most of us work hard to accomplish things that will bring us rewards that we deserve. The danger in contingent joy is its seductiveness. We can be lulled into believing that the only joy we can experience comes from making things happen. The risk is that we will identify contingent joy not only as the best but also as the only kind of joy worth seeking. And when it evades us, as it frequently does, we can sink into a depression that admits no other type of joy.

Contextual Joy

Contextual joy is associated with a set of circumstances that develop over a relatively long period of time. It arises from the context of our life. When a significant area of our life, like work or family, is going well over a period of time, we feel satisfied with life. Contextual joy is concerned with our achievements, goals we have set, our standards and values. It is connected with a feeling of self-efficacy. We experience this level of joy when we view ourselves as having worthy and consistent goals and believing that we have the capacity to carry out our strategies to accomplish those goals. Contextual joy is a companion to high self-esteem and self-respect.

Brad is a client of mine whose life illustrates contextual joy. The son of a successful professional man, Brad became a musician. For the first fifteen years of his adult life, he traveled with a small band playing one-night stands in a long series of half-empty honky-tonks. Alcohol and cocaine hooked him. He became depressed and twice attemped suicide. He chalked up a string of minor brushes with the law for drunk driving and passing hot checks and once spent thirty days in jail for breaking a man's arm during a drunken brawl in a bar. His life was out of control, an undistinguished spinning world punctuated with three marriages and four children.

Finally, his addictions became so severe that his band left him and he woke up in a hotel with no money, no friends, and no family. He didn't even know where he was. Somehow, Brad stumbled into an AA meeting. He got sober and started putting his life back together. He finished his bachelor's degree, became certified as a chemical dependency counselor, and began work on his master's degree.

In the last few years, Brad has opened up to a deeper side of himself. His paternal grandfather was a full-blooded Cherokee Indian whom Brad had never known. He found himself drawn to the spirituality and life-philosophy of Native Americans. He has participated in rituals, learned the language, and explored the customs and beliefs. He says there is something in him that pulls him toward this way of life.

Today Brad's life is still not perfect. He doesn't make much money and is still paying off debts incurred during his drinking days. He has relapsed more than once, and his health is not good. He is not married and has trouble with intimacy, although he is courageously facing this part of his life. But he insists that he has a deep satisfaction with where he is and what he is doing with his life. Although he is not proud of what he has done in the past or of the many people he has disappointed and hurt, Brad is content and satisfied with what he has done with himself. He feels good about how he has put his life back together. He is *proud* of himself. That sense of pride and self-respect is the essence of contextual joy.

This level of joy is based on satisfaction and a sense of accomplishment. It is the feeling we have when we think of ourselves as good persons, as compassionate, industrious, sympathetic, or courageous. We feel contextual joy when we see ourselves as a good spouse or friend. It occurs when we feel satisfied with the job we did or the choices we made. Contextual joy is, then, very close to healthy pride and self-respect.

Contextual joy is contentment or peace of mind. We

feel safe and adequate as persons and are satisfied with where we are in life and with the accomplishments we have made. When we have the sense of complete fulfillment of our wishes in a specific area, we have contextual joy.

The experience of contextual joy exceeds by light years the experience of contingent joy; it is much more long-lasting and satisfying. Although it is, like contingent joy, dependent in some sense on the external environment and on good fortune, we do have greater control over it. We work to achieve accomplishments, and our satisfaction comes with our own efforts.

Congruent Joy

Congruent joy is rare in modern-day America, not because it is so difficult to attain but because we have been taught little about what it is and how to obtain it. Other cultures and philosophies, such as those of Native Americans and Orientals, and some forms of spirituality and religion are more accommodating of congruent joy than most people in our society.

Ancient Sanskrit had a special word for this kind of joy: the word *ananda,* which is probably best translated as "self-existent delight." *Ananda* joy does not depend on the satisfaction of particular needs or the fulfillment of specific desires; it simply emerges or rises spontaneously from within.

Congruent joy is completed joy. It is intrinsic joy because those who possess it do so regardless of external circumstances. It belongs to the person regardless of what is happening around or to him or her.

Perhaps the best word for describing congruent joy is *serenity,* a feeling of being undisturbed, calm, and at peace from within. We enjoy a state of equanimity or composure that starts from our center and arises out of interior balance and agreement. Our serenity enables us to bring things together in a spirit of unity and give them meaning. It is not affected by disturbing external conditions. Thus, congruent joy, like serenity, is a characteristic, not a quality that arises from outside events. We feel serene because of who we are, not because of what is happening to us or because of what we have accomplished. Lao Tzu, the ancient Chinese philosopher, had this in mind when he wrote in *The Way of Life,* "The way to do is to be." When we value who we are beyond what we have achieved or what fortune brings to our door, we have a peaceful, inner calm.

Viktor Frankl is a Holocaust survivor who discovered while in Auschwitz that the Nazis could kill the external self but they could not touch what was inside. He learned and wrote eloquently about how to find unbelievable serenity and meaning under the most inhumane and inhospitable conditions imaginable. Frankl discovered, and teaches us, that to live is to suffer and to survive is to find meaning and worth in our suffering. He is saying that if we have a *why* in life, we can make it through almost any *how.*

In "The God's Script," the Latin-American writer Jorge Luis Borges both defines congruent joy and describes its mysterious manifestations. A prisoner awakes from his dreams of freedom to find himself still trapped behind the impregnable dungeon walls. Somehow he finds the will to be grateful for life even in the "harsh prison." He blessed the dampness, the "crevice of light," and the "darkness and the stone." He even blessed his "old, suffering body." Finally, he concludes, "there occurred what I cannot forget nor communicate. There occurred the union with divinity, with the universe."

Frederick Franck, in his book *The Zen of Seeing: Seeing/ Drawing as Meditation,* describes a mystical experience during his youth, which is an episode of congruent joy:

On a dark afternoon—I was ten or eleven—I was walking on a county road, on my left a patch of curly

Kale, on my right some yellowish Brussels Sprouts. I felt a snowflake on my cheek, and from far away in the charcoal-gray sky I saw the slow approach of a snowstorm. I stood still.

Some flakes were now falling around my feet. A few melted as they hit the ground. Others stayed intact. Then I heard the falling of the snow, with the softest hissing sound.

I stood transfixed, listening . . . and knew what can never be expressed: that the natural is supernatural, and that I am the eye that hears and the ear that sees, that what is outside happens in me, that outside and inside are unseparated.

Both Jorge Luis Borges, in the words of an old man, and Frederick Franck, in the experience of his youth, describe a unity, a coalescence of that which is inside and that which is outside. It is a coming-together in harmony and agreement of those inner qualities and all that surrounds us. So integral is the concordance of what is within and what is without that we experience the two as *one*. That is probably what Julian of Norwich meant when she said, "Betwixt God and ourselves there is no between."

In *The Power of Myth,* Joseph Campbell emphasizes how we can be both different from and in union with what surrounds us. He writes that it is a different kind of world when we are out in it with the "little chipmunks and the great owls." At first we experience the forest as filled with "presences, representing forces and powers and magical possibilities of life." These forces are overwhelming even though they are a part of life. They are natural, as we are natural. Then, Campbell says, it all comes together as we find the force "echoing in" us. The resolution comes when we realize that we "are nature."

The total union we can achieve with our environment is what the character Shug had in mind when, in Alice

Walker's book *The Color Purple,* she commentec
knew that if she cut a tree, her arm would bleed.

The experience of this deepest joy may be differe
different seasons of our lives. Levinson's research rev
that young manhood, for example, is concerned wi
"strength, quickness, endurance and output." The middle
years of adulthood become "a season when other qualities
can ripen: wisdom, judiciousness, magnanimity, unsentimental compassion, breadth of perspective, the tragic
sense."

Typically, young adulthood for both women and men
is spent establishing independence and beginning a family.
We leave home, finish school, enter the work force, get
married, and establish an independent household. The
stress of these social and personal transitions are great, at
best. These early years of adulthood require us to disengage
from parents and take responsibility for our own lives and
futures. We must take actions that are competent, preserv-
ing, and task-oriented. Research indicates that we feel the
first fifteen years of adulthood as a period of extreme competition, pressure, and complication. Both sexes feel
frightened and overburdened by the process of establishing
their adulthood.

The first stage of adulthood often ends in what some
refer to as a "midlife crisis." We become aware that time is
running short and that unless we make changes in our
personal relations, in our work, in our spiritual life, and in
ourselves, it will be too late. We realize that the years of
competitive struggle in the area of productivity have not
produced the good life for which we hoped. These realiza-
tions can bring extreme inner turmoil. We open ourselves
to the questions of meaning and authenticity of our lives.
We encounter the specter of self-doubt and have problems
with self-respect.

This midlife period can be a wonderful opportunity.
We can emerge from this struggle with renewed vigor to

face the second half of our lives and with greater capacity to receive joy at its deepest and most meaningful level. We can learn to relax and welcome joy as we assimilate the truth of the old Chinese saying "What you seek, you already possess." We can experience a dramatic drop in feelings of competition and stress. We begin to look for useful purpose and seek to make a meaningful social contribution. Productivity, social comparison, competition, and success measured by material rewards begin to fade in their importance. We start to discover that life is for living, not doing, and we realize that joy is something you are, not something you have one day but not the next.

The three different levels of joy are hierarchical in the sense that one is deeper and more fulfilling than the others. But they are not progressive or sequential. We may experience one or more at the same time, and we may experience one without the others. We do not work our way smoothly from one level to the next. We may seek and actually infrequently experience the happiness of the first level without ever experiencing the serenity of the third level. Or, conversely, we may have the fullest serenity of the third level while our life situation denies us the circumstance of the happiness of the first level's contingent joy.

David M. Griebner has written a wonderful little parable that he entitles "Shadowbound." It is the story of a man who lives trapped in a desert. He is trapped because he follows his shadow each day. Just before sunrise he prepares by turning his back to the east and waiting. When the sun comes up, he starts the journey, following his shadow. Each day he travels a rough oval as he traces the slow crescent of the sun by following the subtle bending of his shadow and ends the day back at the point where he started that morning.

He had been doing this for as long as he could remember, but, although it was familiar, it left him feeling trapped and alone. Sometimes he wondered what it would feel like to face the sun. He longed to see if there were more to the world than the desert.

Then one morning he heard an inner voice that said, "JUST STOP IT." He knew that the voice referred to following his shadow. But that seemed too simple and, to tell the truth, too foreboding. There was joy and hope in the message of the voice, but there was also fear and dread, because following his shadow was all he knew.

Although he wanted to, he couldn't make himself stop that day. But as he followed his shadow for the next several days he thought about the message of the voice and the freedom that it promised him.

Then one morning he did it. He suddenly turned his face to the sun as it came up in the east. The rising sun was brighter and more wonderful than he had ever imagined. That first day, and for the next several days, he could not move. All he could do was stand there and look around and watch the sun cut across the sky. But he was less and less aware of his shadow.

Finally, one morning he took a step, then another. He fixed his gaze on the mountains in the distance and set out. He didn't know where he was going, but he was not trapped by his own shadow, and he no longer felt alone.

The question is, Where are we? What shadows trap us, and what shadows do we follow? How much joy do we have, and what may we do to open our lives to the deepest and most meaningful experiences of joy?

Chapter 4

ℳEASURING JOY

Life can only be understood backwards; but it must
be lived forwards.

—SØREN KIERKEGAARD

❖ *We have all seen variations*
on the cartoon that shows the beginning of a family vaca-
tion. Everybody is crammed into a packed car, kids screaming and hanging out the windows. A big dog is crowding
the front seat, and luggage is tied precariously on the roof
of the car. Clothing hangs out of the trunk, and a bicycle is
chained to the bumper. One parent painfully inquires, "Are
we having fun yet?"

Most of us lack the ability to know when we are joyful.
That may sound strange, but it is true. We are much more
conscious of our *unhappiness* and of what we do *not* want in
our lives than we are of the joyful and happy particulars.

A friend of mine, Randy McBroom, is a psychotherapist
who told me of the following experience with a client, a
mother of three small children. Her whole life revolved
around her family and church. She had married her high
school sweetheart almost immediately after graduation. Her
three babies came in rapid succession, and all she had time
to do was change diapers, clean house, and go to church.
She was tired all the time.

Dr. McBroom began to help her relax and find time for
herself. After several weeks of therapy, she proudly told him

of taking her son's skateboard and trying it out in her garage. She liked it, and soon she was outside on the driveway, swishing one way and another. She became very excited and started up and down the sidewalk and finally went around the block several times. She smiled and swayed as she related the story to my friend.

"That's wonderful," he responded. "And what do you call the feeling you had on the skateboard?" he asked. She looked blankly at him searching for the correct word. Nothing came. "I guess I don't know," she reluctantly replied. My friend smiled and said, "You call that F-U-N and J-O-Y." They both laughed.

Another woman who is a friend of mine shared with me some of the experiences she had during her visits with a therapist. She was a rigid and controlling person who lived in fear of rejection and failure. Her therapist told her, among many other things, to try to have some fun. "I didn't know what to do," she told me, "because I didn't have the foggiest what fun was."

I know how the these women felt. More than once I have had something good happen in my life and what I felt, rather than happiness, was confusion. We do not know how to recognize joy even as we are experiencing it.

The questions we need to answer are these: How can we tell when we are having joy? Why are we having fun? And, why are we not having fun?

The Characteristics of Joy

If we are ever to recognize joy in our lives, we must first know what it looks like in ourselves and in others. In other words, if joy were a disease, what would its symptoms be?

The following list gives eleven characteristics that I believe to be inherent in joy. Not all are necessarily present at any one time.

- Our thoughts and feelings are spontaneous and free rather than responses to other people's expectations or our own inner fear of not being good.
- We enjoy the moment instead of anticipating future pleasure or living in our past experience of fun.
- We are less judgmental of ourselves and others and are less critical in general.
- Sudden irritability, sadness, and fear are less prominent in our lives.
- We smile and laugh more. Commonplace events offer a sense of pleasure whereas thrills, escapism, and spectator experiences lose their appeal.
- We feel content with our lives. We find ourselves saying, "I like my life" and "I like me."
- We want other people to have a good life, too.
- We appreciate and feel grateful for simple things.
- We feel love for and connectedness with others and nature.
- We let go more. We are willing to let things happen. We do not try to make them happen, and we do not require a specific outcome in every situation in order to be happy.
- We spend less and less time comparing ourselves to others, concentrating on how much we have, or thinking about what we are getting in contrast to them.

If joy were a disease, would you have it? Or, if it were a crime, would there be enough evidence to convict you? We can use this list of characteristics to understand better what is going on in our lives. Take a few moments to consider your life over the last few months or weeks. How many of these characteristics do you acknowledge as you contemplate your life? How many of them are *never* present, and how many only in specific circumstances?

A Joy Test

The following is a list of questions that you may answer to rate your joy quotient. Simply check either *yes* or *no* to the left of each question. Consider each question carefully and answer with what is generally true of your life today. Instructions for scoring the test and interpreting your score are given at the end of the test.

Yes _____ No _____   1. I must plan everything very carefully in order to be comfortable.

Yes _____ No _____   2. I know my needs.

Yes _____ No _____   3. Things must go according to my plan, or else I get uncomfortable.

Yes _____ No _____   4. I feel okay asking for my needs to be met.

Yes _____ No _____   5. I worry that I can never get other people to accept me.

Yes _____ No _____   6. I like taking care of my sexual needs.

Yes _____ No _____   7. I must be in charge of things, or else I feel out of place.

Yes _____ No _____   8. I believe there is no one exactly like me.

Yes _____ No _____   9. I feel uncomfortable with my sexuality.

Yes _____ No _____ 10. I'm glad I am me.

Yes _____ No _____ 11. Frequently when I smile or laugh, it is fake.

Yes _____ No _____ 12. I am comfortable with my place in the world.

Yes _____ No _____ 13. Most of the time I am not content being me.

Yes _____ No _____ 14. I like and accept my body.

Yes _____ No _____ 15. I dislike the "simple things of life."

Yes _____ No _____ 16. I like and accept myself exactly as I am even while I want to change.

Yes _____ No _____ 17. I spend a lot of time in escapist activities like TV, spectator sports, or other activities designed to get my mind off things.

Yes _____ No _____ 18. I am aware of my uniqueness.

Yes _____ No _____ 19. I dislike my life as it is.

Yes _____ No _____ 20. I have a satisfactory sense of the spiritual dimension of my life.

Yes _____ No _____ 21. I am driven to succeed, and yet I do not enjoy the accomplishments I make.

Yes _____ No _____ 22. I am glad I am a woman (or man).

Yes _____ No _____ 23. I dislike most of my friends.

Yes _____ No _____ 24. I have someone with whom I can share my deepest secrets and dreams.

Yes _____ No _____ 25. I often wake up at night and can't get back to sleep.

Yes _____ No _____ 26. I regularly escape from the world and enter into my inner self through some method like meditation, prayer, or hobby.

Yes _____ No _____ 27. I hate the work I do.

Yes _____ No _____ 28. I love my life.

Yes _____ No _____ 29. I sometimes wish I had never been born.

Yes _____ No _____ 30. When I get old and look back on my life as I am living it now, I will have a feeling of peace and satisfaction.

Yes _____ No _____ 31. I have trouble accomplishing the goals I set for myself.

Yes _____ No _____ 32. I sincerely believe that most people like me.

Yes _____ No _____ 33. I frequently feel helpless and lost.

Yes _____ No _____ 34. I look forward to each new day.

Yes _____ No _____ 35. Often I think that others have a better life than I do.

Yes _____ No _____ 36. I am excited about life.

Yes _____ No _____ 37. I find it hard to forget my mistakes and get on with it.

Yes _____ No _____ 38. I am an enthusiastic person.

Yes _____ No _____ 39. I criticize myself most of the time.

Yes _____ No _____ 40. I feel that I make a contribution to the world.

Yes _____ No _____ 41. I dislike sex.

Yes _____ No _____ 42. I know that I am special to someone.

Yes _____ No _____ 43. I have no close friends.

Yes _____ No _____ 44. I feel good about my genitals.

Yes _____ No _____ 45. No one really knows me.

Yes _____ No _____ 46. I am comfortable with my body weight.

Yes _____ No _____ 47. I believe that most people, when they get to know me, will not like me.

Yes _____ No _____ 48. I feel that I have worthwhile goals for my life.

Yes _____ No _____ 49. My life is largely a failure.

Yes _____ No _____ 50. I like the way I am sexually.

SCORING THE TEST Give yourself two points for each *yes* answer to the even-numbered questions and two points for each *no* answer to the odd-numbered questions. Add all the numbers together; that is your score on the test.

INTERPRETING YOUR SCORE

85–100	Excellent	Deep serenity and contentment in life
70–84	Good	Life satisfaction is acceptable, but some areas need attention
50–69	Poor	Little sense of joy in life
Below 50	Troubled	Joy is largely absent

The test contains six subsets of questions. A table for determining your score for each subset is provided below. To use the tables, please record your scores to each question in the space after the number for each question. Use the same even and odd numbering method described above. (For example, in the first subset, "General Life Satisfaction," if you answered *no* to question no. 2, write a 0 in the blank; and if you answered *yes* to question no. 4, write a 2 in the appropriate blank below.) When you have written the correct scores, total each subset in the appropriate space. That total is your score for that subset.

GENERAL LIFE SATISFACTION

Questions	2 _____	17–20	Excellent
	4 _____	13–16	Good
	6 _____	10–12	Poor
	11 _____	Below 10	Troubled
	17 _____		
	19 _____		
	28 _____		
	30 _____		
	34 _____		
	36 _____		
Total	_____		

SELF-WORTH ISSUES

Questions	5 ____	17–20	Excellent
	8 ____	13–16	Good
	10 ____	10–12	Poor
	16 ____	Below 10	Troubled
	18 ____		
	29 ____		
	32 ____		
	37 ____		
	38 ____		
	39 ____		
Total	____		

CONTROL ISSUES

Questions	1 ____	10–12	Excellent
	3 ____	8–9	Good
	7 ____	6–7	Poor
	25 ____	Below 6	Troubled
	33 ____		
	49 ____		
Total	____		

RELATIONSHIPS

Questions	23 ____	10–12	Excellent
	24 ____	8–9	Good
	42 ____	6–7	Poor
	43 ____	Below 6	Troubled
	45 ____		
	47 ____		
Total	____		

BODY IMAGE AND SEXUALITY

Questions	6 _____	14–16	Excellent
	9 _____	11–13	Good
	14 _____	8–10	Poor
	22 _____	Below 8	Troubled
	41 _____		
	44 _____		
	46 _____		
	50 _____		
Total	_____		

VOCATION AND OCCUPATION ISSUES

Questions	12 _____	12–14	Excellent
	21 _____	9–11	Good
	27 _____	7–8	Poor
	31 _____	Below 7	Troubled
	35 _____		
	40 _____		
	48 _____		
Total	_____		

After you have finished scoring the test and interpreted your scores, look back over the test. Consider the following questions:

1. Which questions really stand out in your mind?
   Select five questions that stand out in some unusual way for you.
   What do your answers to these specific questions
   mean to you?
   Write out a brief explanation of what is significant about each for you.
2. How do you feel about your overall score? What
   about your scores on the subsets? Were there any
   surprises to you concerning your scores?
3. Select three words that describe where you are with

reference to joy in your life. Write those words in the space below.

4. What do you want to change in your life as you consider your responses to this test?
   List five things you wish to change in your life.

   What specific actions will you take to begin making these changes in your life?
5. Please consider sharing your answers to these questions with some person whom you can trust.

My kittens know how to be happy. They do not need this chapter, and they don't need to take a test. It comes naturally. They roll and turn and stretch and run and roll again. They find incalculable pleasure in a small leaf, which they push and throw and chase. They cannot conceal their fascination with a string—until, without warning, their concentration shifts to a tiny bug, which they follow with unmitigated curiosity. They leap over small plants and hide, stalking one another, then spring with mock ferocity on each other. And, above all, they chase their own tails with endless, unself-conscious delight. Kathy K. Grow's poem captures what kitten joy is about:

Exult, O God!
Exult with Walter in the wonder of his tail!
Tips and turns,
Loops-the-loop,
Somersaults
Through mid-air:
Look with joy
At kitten's discovered delight,

80

And exult, O God, in your gift,
The gift of Walter's tail!

Exult, O God!
Exult with Walter in the wonder of his tail!
Preened and washed,
Carefully shaped
Around his nose
And over his paws:
Look with joy
At kitten's exhausted delight,
And exult, O God, in your gift,
The gift of Walter's tail.

In a sour moment Samuel Johnson, the great eighteenth-century British thinker, said, "Life is a progress from want to want, not from enjoyment to enjoyment." Let us hope that he was just having a bad day when he said that. But, who knows? His assessment of life may have been true for him. His evaluation does not have to be correct for us today. We can do better than go from want to want.

It is, of course, true that we are all novices at life. Every time we begin to get it right, we move on to something new. Just as we get comfortable with one stage, we move to the next one. We are like a concert pianist who is learning a piece of music at the same time that she is playing it in recital. Maybe that is what Mark Twain meant when he said that life would probably be happier if we could be born at the age of eighty and gradually approach eighteen.

We do move from want to want. But there can be enjoyment along the way as we learn to chase our own tails. Not knowing where our next step will take us can be joy.

Chapter 5

❖

The Anatomy
of Joy

Peace comes within the souls of [people] when they
realize their oneness with the universe.

—Black Elk

❖ *In November 1991, the doc-*
tors told Mary Schramski that her father was dying. Jim
Hauser, a seventy-two-year-old former airline pilot, had a
malignant tumor on his spine. His prognosis for recovery
was very poor. His physicians gave him only a few months
to live, at best, and they prescribed radiation treatment and
many pain killers.

Mary, a community college teacher in Keller, Texas,
had spent most of her life separated from her father and did
not know him very well. She did know that he had not been
sick a day in his life and that he had been very careful with
his nutrition and exercise. For many years he had run ten
miles a day, and as he grew older he had reduced his exercise to walking. She resolved to spend as much time with
him as possible during the last days of his life. She resigned
her position and traveled back and forth between her home
and where her father lived in Las Cruces, New Mexico. She
was with him throughout the radiation treatments, and she
personally monitored his medication each day.

As predicted by his physicians, his condition worsened. By early January, he refused to eat, would not voluntarily get out of bed, and was deeply depressed. He weighed only 104 pounds and was catheterized. He had lost all hope and had no interest in life. Mary believed that he was ready to die.

In February, she decided to take him home with her. "I wanted my father to die in my home," she explained. His physicians protested that he was too weak to make the trip. But Mary insisted.

Mary resolved to do two things during her father's last days. She would make him as comfortable as possible, and she would do everything she could to get to know as much about him as she could. She spent virtually every minute of the day with him. They talked and shared their lives with each other. She saw to it that some time was spent outdoors every day. She took him places and found things for him to do to help her. But mostly they talked.

Mary altered the medication plan that the doctors had prescribed. Instead of giving her father a handful of pain-killers and sedatives every two hours, she waited until he asked for them. His requests came farther and farther apart. He began to feel better. He started spending more time out of bed. He went three days without any pain medication. He seemed more alert. He could not get enough of his conversations with Mary. He began to speak of the future. "I *made* him have hope," Mary joyfully explained.

Her father didn't die. He is back to his walking, has a hearty appetite, and is once again careful about eating nutritiously. He returned to Las Cruces and sold his property there. He bought a lot in Keller and built a home for himself. Today he is alert and interested in life, and he and Mary are still getting to know each other.

How do we explain what happened to this man? No one knows for sure. The radiation treatments may have "cured" the cancer, and Mr. Hauser simply got well. Or perhaps the radiation did its job and, in combination with the medication, kept him alive throughout his recovery period until his body got strong enough to recuperate. Or, it's possible that Mr. Hauser was dying because he did not care about living, and something happened to give him hope and a reason to live. Hope and purpose encouraged his brain and body to turn around. His brain sent "live messages" to his body instead of "die messages," and Mr. Hauser got well in mind and body.

What exactly happened in Mr. Hauser's brain and body is, to be sure, open to speculation. But what happened to his life and feelings is not. How are our emotions connected to the rest of our life, and how do they affect what happens to us in body, mind, and spirit?

Joy and Body-Mind-Spirit Health

Which of the following is hardest to do?

Give up an addiction
Initiate and stick with a diet
Begin and sustain an exercise program
Develop a new hobby
Find a new and better job
Develop new feelings about yourself

If you answered "develop new feelings about yourself," then you are correct. The hardest thing for us to do is to change the way we feel about ourselves. The Campbell Soup Company and *American Health* recently sponsored an extensive Gallup survey of over one thousand people nationwide that was designed to answer questions about the hows and whys of change. They were interested in determining what gets us going and how long our changes last. They wanted to know what kind of changes were hardest for us and what helps us develop new behaviors and new ways of seeing ourselves. They asked about what sustains changes as well as what makes us quit after we have begun a change.

As reported by Judith Hurley and Richard Schlaadt in *The Wellness Life-Style,* the survey found that the hardest changes people make are internal and have to do with feelings. Over half of the respondents said that emotional changes were more demanding than changing behaviors. They rated emotional change as "difficult," and roughly a third of those interviewed said that it was "the hardest thing I have ever done."

Fear and self-disgust, feelings about their bodies and competence, understanding and dealing with their anger, and changing feelings about their lack of self-confidence and sense of self-worth are the types of inner changes with which these respondents had difficulty. In comparison, outward changes of behavior and habit were easy.

The survey also determined that despite the struggle required, emotional change was worth the effort because making an inner change has a positive ripple effect. Approximately two-thirds of the respondents reported that once they changed this aspect of their lives they wanted to change other aspects, too. Further, the survey determined that emotional patterns are important in another regard: if we are to maintain outward life changes—for example, new eating habits, new hobbies, new exercise programs, new jobs—we must *first* change our feelings. Emotional changes must accompany life-style changes if these changes are to be more than temporary. Unless outward changes are accompanied by appropriate inner changes, we are not be able to maintain new life-styles indefinitely.

There is no doubt that emotions make an impact on the body and, conversely, that the body affects the emotions. In fact, the relationship between the mind and the body is so strong that they may no longer be thought of as two separate entities. In his book *Rediscovering the Soul*, Larry Dossey quotes Candace Pert, a neuropharmacologist and the former Chief of Brain Chemistry at the National Institute of Health: "I can no longer make a strong distinction between the brain and the body." And again, "the research findings . . . indicate that we need to start thinking about how consciousness can be projected into various parts of the body."

Thus, from a scientific point of view, it is no longer appropriate to separate the body from the mind. Nor, in my thinking, may we separate the two from the spirit. We are not speaking correctly when we say that we are a mind that has a body attached to it and that perhaps a spirit exists somewhere. The trichotomy of body, mind, and soul divides one part of ourselves from another. It is a concept in need of rethinking. We are a body-mind-spirit; an interconnected and interrelated set of parts that support and mutually affect one another. No one part by itself is complete, and no one section is superior to the other. As St. Paul said centuries ago, "The eye may not say to the hand, 'I have no need of you.' " No one function is any more or less important than any other. Feelings are not optional and cannot be put away like a useless old coat that we no longer wear. Feelings are real, and they have an impact on everything else in our lives.

Bernie Siegel, a physician who works with cancer patients, writes enthusiastically of the impact of feelings on the health and well-being of his patients. In *Peace, Love, and Healing* he states, "Feelings are chemical and can kill or cure." He insists that a sense of joy and peace and general optimism about life contribute to health in every area of being, as well as longevity. On the other hand, a state of learned helplessness, in which individuals feel hopeless, with no control over events or stress in their lives, is associated with poor health.

What all this means is that our physical as well as psychological well-being is dependent on how we look at ourselves and at life. On the one hand, research leaves no doubt that our genetic makeup and our physical environment influence our vulnerability to physical disease and mental disorders. On the other hand, the evidence is equally conclusive that our internal emotional world is a trigger that activates mechanisms of either health or infirmity.

Loving Ourselves with a Whole Love

The question is, How do we see ourselves? In *Letters to a Young Poet,* Rainer Maria Rilke once advised a young friend, "What is going on in your innermost being is worthy of your whole love." What is this whole love? I do not know precisely what Rilke meant by the term. His mystical wisdom and understanding of life far exceed my own. But I know what the term means to me. To me, whole love speaks of a gentle patience and encouraging self-acceptance. When I love myself with a whole love, I do not hold up an account of my failures, of how far I fall short of my humanity, of how limited I am in my being. Whole love is not conditional about any aspect of my innermost being.

A whole love helps us to remember that it is only when we give ourselves permission to fail that we have any real hope of success. Burt Rutan, aviation designer, put it like this: "Only the place that tolerates failure gives rise to the thinking that results in success." Conditional acceptance and intolerant thinking are not whole love.

WHOLE LOVE JOINS THE MIND AND HEART We all know that the brain is where thoughts occur. We assume we have one up on Aristotle because he believed that thoughts originate in the heart. We know better. The brain does the thinking, and we "know" things in the brain. And yet, we still speak of "knowing in our hearts." We say things like "I know in my heart that she is right." If we know something in the brain, we know it; but if we "know it in our heart," we *really* know it. More than mere metaphor is at work here. Theophan the Recluse, a nineteenth-century Russian spiritual writer, spoke of the need of descending "with the mind into the heart." When we do, he avers, we pray with the heart and have within us a "small murmuring stream." Something real occurs when our brain and body are connected through the anatomy of joy. Small miracles occur when we love ourselves with this "whole love," and the small murmuring stream, the healing effect that whole love produces, does its life-giving work in us.

BE CAREFUL WHAT YOU SAY WHEN YOU ARE TALKING TO YOURSELF Consider just one small and unimportant aspect of the need to love ourselves: the phrases and terms that we use to describe and explain ourselves in our everyday experience. Some people refer to inner language as "self-talk," others call it "roof-brain chatter," whereas still others designate it our "chatterbox." "Inner tapes" and "core dialogue" are two other terms that have been used to describe the interior editorializing in which we are constantly involved.

Whatever the term we use, the content of this language falls into two categories: for some of us the language is self-defeating; it is a language of limits, of defeat, loss, and failure. This language lowers self-esteem and sends a "you should die" message to the body. It encourages punitive and fearful messages and images. It lowers stamina and blocks energy and shuts out all feelings of joy. It is negative in tone, and self-defeat is the primary theme of these patterns. They form an endlessly judgmental harangue that becomes a self-fulfilling prophecy.

For others the interior conversation is built on a language that uplifts both the self and others. It is the language of joy, confidence, and worth. It encourages images of accomplishment and value. It avoids words of success and failure, words that basically compare us to others and put us in a win-lose situation. Rather, it is based on noncompetitive language.

Consider, as an example, a student who is struggling with a heavy load and is in danger of being overwhelmed by her studies. She will help herself with affirmations like "There is time for me to do what I need to do," "I can learn what I need for life," or "I am strong and capable and can do what I need to do." She will not help herself if she tries to make herself believe affirmations like "I have the best brain in this university" or "I am smarter than anyone in my class." The latter are competitive and comparative and require her to beat everyone else rather than simply be the best she can be.

Or consider a man who is struggling with self-hatred that includes an ugly body image. This person will not help himself by declaring that his is the most beautiful body in the world. The words "most beautiful" keep him externally referenced and competing with others. These affirmations have the effect of *increasing* the pressure to change his body according to some external standard. Further, the mind is not fooled by these shallow statements. It recognizes a lie when it hears one. Rather, more constructive affirmations are "My body is okay as it is" and "It's okay for me to be me."

The language of joy gives a "you deserve to live" message to the body. It encourages health and well-being in the mind and body and soul. It empowers us to meditate on higher themes and give ourselves positive messages, and it guides our minds toward constructive images. And it, like its more negative variety, becomes a self-fulfilling prophecy.

We engage daily in this inner dialogue. We address ourselves overtly by the names we call ourselves and the labels we place on ourselves. These self-imposed tags are important in determining the attitude we have about what is going on in our environment and our self-feelings about how we deal with that environment. The language we use forms the basis of the "mental set" that exists in our thinking. This set contains basic themes or patterns of thought that are like tape recordings that play in the background. These habitual patterns form an internal environment or "overvoice" that evaluates each action and dictates our own emotional response to how we are doing at life. It forms either an upward cycle that encourages positive feelings, and thus a sense of accomplishment, or a downward cycle that fosters the opposite.

The Old Testament reminds us, "He who guards his mouth saves his life." Listen to your inner language. Where you observe it to be negative and life-threatening, be prepared to change it.

Let me give a simple example of how we can change our inner language. Once, when I worked in a psychiatric hospital, I gave a group of men who were in my care an assignment to write a list of affirmations about themselves. I explained that affirmations are things that are *positive* and *true* about ourselves that we may say to ourselves daily to improve the way we feel about ourselves and our ability to make it in the world.

The next day in our group therapy session we talked about what we had written and how we could use it for guidance and strength. One man who suffered deep depression did not say a word. After the session, I found the following list on the chair that this man had occupied.

AFFIRMATIONS FOR ME

by Bill C.

I am a precious child of God.
I am a handsome man.
I am worth good health.

I am a man who has wants and needs, and that's okay.
I am a useful person who has lots of beauty and gifts
to share with others.
I'm so glad I'm here.
I'm so glad I'm a man.
I'm worth being heard.
I am in touch with the precious child in me.
I am a worthwhile person.
I am a precious human being worthy of dignity and
respect.
I am a man who accepts others as they are without
trying to change them to meet my needs.
I am a man who is in touch with my feelings and
attitudes about every aspect of my life, including
my sexuality.
I accept myself fully, even while wanting to change
parts of myself.
I am able to get my needs met.
I am responsible for only myself.
I am worth knowing.
I am lovable.
I am strong and confident.
I am able to take risks with appropriate people.
I accept not being in control at times; I am still okay.
I am an intelligent person.
I utilize my intelligence at work.
I affirm me and my right to live.

I think this is a wonderful list of affirmations. Within
each statement is the strength to move toward ourselves, a
self-attitude rooted in kindly, peaceful self-acceptance.
When we can truly say these things about ourselves, we will
feel safe and compassionate toward ourselves.

WHOLE LOVE MEANS WE DON'T
NEED TO KEEP SECRETS When we accept
what we are with whole love, and when we affirm that

which we are, we no longer need to hide the truth. That simple fact means, first, that we can look directly and honestly at what we are. Next, it means that if we choose, we can share openly and without shame what we are with those persons we trust. Finally, it means that we need never fear the criticism of other people.

Virtually all the clients I work with come to me with large parts of themselves that they feel they must keep hidden. These persons spend much energy trying to protect themselves from what they fear will be negative consequences if they let other people see what they are.

They have good reason for this behavior, or so they think. Most of them have lived a life of fear of being found defective and being abandoned by the people they need and love. As they come to respect what they genuinely are and to love themselves with a whole love, they learn that they do not have to hide. They usually learn that lesson through the painful experience of sharing those things that they think are so negative about themselves. They tell their secrets and find that the secrets no longer have power over them. They do not die, and neither does anyone else. They find out that the things they are saying to themselves in all those affirmations are true, after all. They find that they *are* okay!

At Home in Our Own House

What is the anatomy of emotion? Or, how is it that an emotional state can cause a physical ailment in the body or a psychological disorder in the mind? How does the brain work and how does it communicate with itself and with the body?

TAKING CARE OF OURSELVES IN A THREAT A good place to start such a discussion is to look at what happens in our brain and our body when we perceive some threat to our well-being. Let's say, for example, that a person thinks that her boss is about to ridicule her for a mistake she made at work. This experience sets in motion a complex chemical process within her that affects her entire being.

The first physical reaction occurs in the limbic region of the brain. The limbic, located at the midsection of the brain and slightly smaller than a fist, is the seat of our emotions. As the brain registers the ridicule she expects the boss to inflict, the hypothalamus, a grape-sized organ at the bottom of the limbic region, immediately produces a chemical messenger called corticotropin-releasing factor (CRF). CRF's main function is to stimulate what is called the fight or flight mechanism, a reaction that evolved long ago to help us and other species respond quickly to threatening situations.

CRF stimulates the sympathetic nerves that are connected to all organs and arteries throughout the body. The chemical messenger used for this process is called norepinephrine, a neurotransmitter associated with arousal and moods. Simultaneously, CRF alerts the pituitary gland, another part of the limbic system, to send a message to the adrenal glands, sitting atop the kidneys, to release a cluster of stress hormones, including adrenaline. These chemicals flood the body and bring about a range of responses, each of which is designed to help the person cope with the threat from the environment.

As these chemicals race through the body, a number of physiological changes occur. The rate and strength of the heartbeat increase, which allows oxygen to be pumped more rapidly and in greater quantity into the cells of the muscles. The liver releases stored sugar for use by the muscles. The body shifts the blood supply from the skin and viscera to irrigate the muscles and brain. Respiration increases, and blood pressure and blood volume are increased to help seal wounds. Moisture is drawn from the skin and mouth for use by the brain, which explains why our mouth goes dry when we are under pressure.

B R A I N - T A L K   The limbic sends chemical messages to the cerebrum, the unit of the brain that controls sensory, associative, and motor operations and is the site of higher mental functions such as memory and reasoning. The cerebrum is composed of two large masses or hemispheres, each of which is wrinkled and grooved and resembles, in the words of Richard Restak in *The Brain,* a "soft, wrinkled walnut." The cerebrum sits like a thick umbrella over and around the limbic and is the seat of our rational and cognitive abilities. Chemical and electrical impulses from the limbic stimulate various lobes of the cerebrum. The cerebrum responds to these messages by producing thoughts that define and explain what is happening in the environment. Even as our body is responding to the threat, our cerebrum is trying to make sense of it all and fit what is happening into logical categories. Chemicals from the cerebrum act as further messages that restimulate the limbic and continue the cycle of mutual interaction of the brain and the body.

This complicated process is a wonderful and necessary survival mechanism. When we are confronted with danger such as a personal attack or an imminent automobile accident or a falling object, our brain and body combine harmoniously and instantaneously in an effort to save our life. But what happens when this internal activity is chronic? That is, what happens to us when we live with the hypothalamus continually sending messages across the body that the environment contains a serious threat to our survival? What happens to us when a little adrenaline is constantly seeping into our system? What, for example, is going on in a person whose constant response to life is anxiety, hostility, suspicion, or a desire for control? What is the effect on body and mind and spirit when one's body is constantly flooded with stress hormones as if all of life were a constant threat?

Beth, one of my clients, is a good example of a person whose reaction to life keeps her body surging with stress hormones. Beth is a quiet person who has a peaceful and serene exterior. She is about forty-five, the mother of two grown daughters, and has been married to the same man for approximately twenty-five years. Raised in a very strict religious home, Beth has struggled with her faith over the years. Her marriage is not personally fulfilling, and she has many times thought of divorce. But her religion forbids divorce, and she is not secure in her ability to provide financially for herself.

Beth works as a legal secretary in a small law firm in her community. Although she is very competent at work, she does not feel comfortable and generally believes that her superiors find her inadequate. To complicate the matter at work, she lacks good people skills and doesn't feel that she fits in with her fellow workers. She seeks to please everyone and tries hard not to rock the boat.

One day, without warning, her boss announced that she had been transferred to another department. Her responsibilities remained the same, but she had a new supervisor. She maintained the outward image of composure and competence. Inside she was overwhelmed with fear that her new boss would expect too much, change her job so that it was impossible for her, or simply fire her and replace her with someone he liked better.

Beth constantly felt tired. Her back and neck hurt all the time. She had trouble sleeping and gained weight. She tried everything her physician suggested. She took sleeping pills and antidepressants and even self-prescribed alcohol. Nothing worked.

Beth and I began to work on altering how she felt about herself and how she saw her world. She responded, and everything began to change and her symptoms began to fade. Up until these internal changes took place, Beth's feelings of personal worthlessness pulled her downward into a negative spiral toward physical and emotional breakdown. Ultimately, her system would have collapsed in response to the burden she placed on it.

The Chemistry of Joy

Is it possible to tap into the body's and brain's natural propensity toward health? Can we use our internal processes to heal and even prevent both physical and psychological disorders? Much research says that we can.

HOPE AS HEALER   The Old Testament contains the sage advice, "A merry heart doeth good like a medicine; but a broken spirit drieth the bones." According to this wise proverb, feeling joy and expressing it has a positive effect on us. Laughter is good for us, and happiness and hope and love are physically and psychologically beneficial. They work like good medicine.

Consider laughter. We laugh almost as early as we cry. Most likely, you started laughing when you were two and one-half months old. By four months, you were laughing about once an hour, and by four years of age, you were laughing once every four minutes. But this trend toward increasing laughter that started early in life gets reversed. Laughter decreases in adulthood.

Nonetheless, laughing has been shown to be good for us. When we laugh, very positive effects take place in our bodies. A good, hearty belly-laugh raises our body temperature about half a degree and sets our whole cardiovascular system pulsating in a healthy direction. It gently massages the muscles of our abdominal, lumbar, and chest area. It reverberates up our windpipe, banging against the trachea and vibrating in our glottis (the openings between our vocal cords) and our larynx. Finally, it rumbles forth from between our smiling lips at a speed of seventy miles an hour. When it is all over, the muscles of our bodies are relaxed. We *feel* good because our whole system has been touched in a healthy manner.

Norman Cousins, once the editor of *Saturday Review* and formerly Adjunct Professor of Medical Humanities at the UCLA School of Medicine, was diagnosed in 1976 with collagen disease, a life-threatening and crippling disorder. He wrote a book called *Anatomy of an Illness,* which chronicled his efforts to recover from this supposedly irreversible disintegration of his connective tissue. He claimed that laughter was the main element of his recovery. In constant pain, he discovered that after watching Marx Brothers movies and old *Candid Camera* shows he could get a little pain-free sleep. Ten minutes of laughter, he claimed, earned him one hour of untroubled sleep.

He did not claim that his laughter cured his degenerative condition. Laughter for him, rather, was a metaphor for the full range of positive emotions like hope, optimism, faith, love, will to live, capacity for festivity, and purpose and meaning in life. Cousins tapped into the chemistry of joy without knowing fully what he was doing. In his most recent book, *Head First: The Biology of Hope,* he wrote that not much was known then about how the brain worked or how it communicated with the body. In fact, when he first wrote about his laughter therapy, the medical community was skeptical of the entire concept of laughter helping to heal our body and mind.

Since then, a whole new field has emerged that explores the connection of mind and body in the healing process. It is called psychoneuroimmunology. The focuses of this new area of medical study are the relationship of the emotions and healing and the way the mind affects the immune system. There is now no doubt that it does. Scientists today are interested in questions of *how*. How is it possible that laughter and love and joy and optimism and positive thinking can prevent disease and keep us healthy in mind and body?

SKIN HUNGER AND THE BIOLOGY OF HUGGING When I hug my wife, more than just physical contact occurs. I am, of course, doing something symbolic. I am asserting through this act that I love her and that I think she loves me and that I am secure and happy in our relationship. But something more than the symbolic gesture is taking place; a chemical event is also occurring. As I hold her close and feel her body against mine, I actually feel the physiological *rush* of pleasure sweep through my body. Just thinking about holding her close gives me pleasure that I can feel in my body. The body *needs* this experience. So great is the desire of the body for touch that some thinkers liken it to hunger. It is through touch that we first gave and received messages to our environment, and touch is an important method of communication throughout life.

When the brain experiences joy, it sends messages to the body that all is okay with the world. In effect, the brain is saying, Be healthy and happy. The body responds with beneficial responses. The heart reacts with stronger, slower beats and increases blood circulation. Skeletal muscles in the respiratory, abdominal, and facial areas relax. Breathing is deeper, which, along with the increased blood circulation, delivers more oxygen to cells throughout the body. The immune system perks up, and the whole body releases tension. Blair Justice, a psychologist at Texas Health Services in Houston, cites a study in his book *Who Gets Sick* that shows that reacting to something funny results in an increase of antibodies in saliva. Joy reduces adrenalin and other stress hormones. The simple act of smiling, Justice reports, often resets the nervous system so that it reacts less violently to stress. So powerful are these physical effects that just assuming the facial expressions of happiness increases the flow of blood to the brain and stimulates the production of health-giving peptides in the brain. Games, relaxing play, humor that does not come at anyone's expense, singing and dancing, taking a warm bath, crying when hurt, talking to and stroking a pet—all are soul-enhancing, and each helps us release our tight grip on stress.

THE MORPHINE WITHIN   How are we to explain these beneficial effects of joy in our lives? How does the brain make this positive response to feelings of optimism and hope? We now know that any circumstance that, for whatever reason, raises expectations of a positive outcome stimulates the brain to produce a category of neurotransmitters called endorphins. Endorphins are an analgesic; they kill pain and enable the body to heal itself. The word *endorphins* itself is a clue to its function in the body: it combines the first parts of *endogenous,* meaning within, and *morphine,* a painkilling opiate.

There are three categories of endorphins, and laboratory tests have found one of them to be seven hundred times more powerful a painkiller than morphine. These chemicals are, then, very significant as healing agents, and our brains (as well as our entire spinal column and all the nerve endings in our whole body) produce them naturally. When the circumstances, or our attitude toward these circumstances, are right, our entire nervous system can flood the body with these life-enhancing chemicals.

When the brain floods the body with endorphins, we call the result a "natural high" because the sensation is similar to the elation brought about by a drug-induced state. Perhaps the most widely recognized natural high occurs in people who exercise vigorously and regularly. These people often experience a state of euphoria that they call "runner's high."

James Corry and Peter Cimbolic, in their book *Drugs*, have this to say about one jogger who experienced runner's high:

> The highest I have ever been was following a marathon run. At about fifteen miles the run turned into an "experience." It was not one of those things where I was unaware of the pain. The pain was intimate.
>
> Upon completion of the run I was extremely exhausted. Within forty-five minutes I had recovered and began to experience a completely calm feeling. The physical sensations were those of warmth which penetrated my whole body, not just the surface. It felt like my nervous system was undergoing a massage, and my body felt extremely integrated. The mental aspects of this high were calm, clear, extremely lucid thought patterns, almost dreamlike.
>
> I felt that I was at peace with myself and all others. When I looked at strangers, I felt like I saw right through them all the way down to the point inside that was love. Even the oddest of bodies appeared to me as an "angel in disguise." There was no prejudice toward anything or anyone. I felt "in love" with everything and felt a respect and love for all things to the point of crying. It was so extraordinary to see the "sacredness of all things."

I have encouraged my students to discuss their personal experiences of states of altered consciousness produced in natural, non–drug-induced ways. One of them, a strapping, athletic young man named Tom Malooly, told me recently about his experience of bungee-jumping:

> I was filled with fear, almost to the point of paralysis. I had not slept a wink the night before and I didn't think I could get one foot in front of the other. But strangely, I was also excited. My heart was pounding like it was going to jump out of my chest. I felt like I

couldn't breathe and yet I have never felt such capacity to fill my chest with air.

Finally, I got to the jump point. I have a number of gaps in my memory about getting there. But, finally, I was there and I just stood there staring out into space. In that moment, the greatest peace and calm overtook me. I have never felt anything like it before or since. I became the space into which I was about to jump. I can't really explain it. There were people down there who had come to see me jump. But I was not separate from them; I was them. I was the trees and even the dirt toward which I would jump. The sky and clouds were me and I was them. In that moment, I did not really exist as separate from anything else. I was everything and everything was me.

Then, I lifted off and floated outward like in slow motion. I felt nothing but peace and love. It was the most joyful experience of my life. I wanted it never to end.

But exercise and bungee-jumping are not the only methods by which to open ourselves to the body's internal and natural healing systems. Any method that changes the mind and offers the opportunity for altered states of consciousness, that helps us develop self-esteem and a meaning for life, that encourages us to know our value and to revere all living things, is an effective tool to stimulate the body to produce endorphins. Prayer, meditation, visualization, relaxation, acceptance in a support group, awareness, self-hypnosis, psychotherapy, laughter, peaceful interludes of love and joy—all these are methods of increasing endorphins in the body. They all lower blood pressure, slow the heart rate, increase the body's ability to take in oxygen, relax muscles, calm the mind, and reduce stress. Each stimulates the limbic region of the brain to send messages that result in the production of endorphins. Each produces a natural high in its own way.

And, just as impressive, these positive physical and emotional effects are long-lasting. For example, James Pennebaker, a professor of psychology at Southern Methodist University in Dallas, conducted a simple experiment on twenty-five adults. He asked them to write about the traumatic events of their lives. They were instructed simply to put down the details of the disturbing life experiences and describe their feelings about them. He matched these twenty-five persons with an equal-sized control group whose members were told to write about superficial topics. Blood tests given at the experiment's conclusion showed strikingly improved immune functions in the individuals who expressed their feelings about negative events in their lives. Pennebaker called these persons "emoters." The blood tests were repeated after six months, and the positive effects on the immune systems of the emoters were still in effect.

INCREASING YOUR ABILITY TO PRODUCE ENDORPHINS Any of the preceding methods that appeals to you can be an important way to increase endorphins in your system. Select one or more and practice it for a while to determine the effects in your own life. In addition, you may wish to consider including some of the following as habitual parts of your life:

1. Keep a daily journal and record your feelings and dreams. As Pennebaker's study reveals, writing helps.
2. Lighten up a little. Take yourself less seriously. Most of the things we worry about never happen. Learn to relax and do nothing. Don't take your investments or your job or your church or your children so seriously.
3. Laugh a lot. Go looking for things to laugh about. Find things about yourself and life in general to laugh at. Laugh *with* people, never at their expense.

4. Focus on what you want, not what you don't want. Write down what you want from life and what you want to do with your life. Commit yourself to focusing on these goals, not on the negative things that keep you from achieving them. Write out a brief statement of commitment to doing so.

5. When you are ready to do so in a noncritical way, sit or stand naked before a mirror and draw a picture of your body. Record your feelings and thoughts about your body. Work with the negative feelings that come up. Write a letter of appreciation to your body for all the things it has done for you over the years.

6. Make affirmations. Select one affirmation a day and, at least fifteen times a day, say it aloud to yourself.

7. Find time for play at least fifteen minutes a day. Take a walk or do other aerobic exercises for twenty minutes, five times a week. Take time off from your responsibilities. Rest and relax with what is fun for you.

8. Eat healthfully. Reduce or eliminate junk foods and drugs from your dietary intake. If you do not wish to eliminate drugs and junk food from your intake, stipulate specifically in writing how much you will take in each day. Write about the times you struggle with your decision.

9. Find a group in which you can share the truth about yourself. If you can't do it with your family, find a "family of choice." If you are afraid, do it anyway.

10. Meditate, visualize, pray, or listen to quiet music for at least two fifteen-minute periods each day. If you do not know how to do these things, find someone who does, and ask him or her to teach you.

To help you with meditation, consider trying the following visualization:

Sit comfortably with your eyes closed, and focus on your breathing. When you are nice and relaxed, let your mind picture a sunrise. See the light moving slowly across the landscape toward you. Reach your hands out toward the sun, and see the light touch your fingers. Feel the light gently enter your body and move slowly up and down until your whole being is illuminated. Feel the healing warmth of the light, and let it make your body and mind and spirit whole.

See yourself peacefully surrounded by a warm glow. This is the power of life and the force that created you. Visualize yourself connected with your creator. Let the power and love of that connection move into your body. Give yourself an affirming message such as "I am a valuable, special, and strong person."

Now go more deeply inside yourself to the place of your greatest fear and hurt. See the wounds of pain and hurt that have accumulated over the years. Gently touch that part of yourself, and see the light move slowly across the raw and broken parts. Feel the healing warmth and loving touch. Give yourself the affirming message "I am finding healing and strength in all the broken parts of my life."

Locate the place where you keep your most precious treasure. This is your most sacred place because it is here that the essence of you abides. As you approach this hallowed place, be aware, first, of all those who have loved and helped you. See their faces, and then see yourself walk up to each and tell them how they have helped you. Thank each one, then move on to the next. Then, see all your resources: your ability to love, see, hear, speak, touch, taste, feel, think, move, and choose. Linger at each of these resources, and remember how you have used them and how they have served you. Remember that these resources are a part of you and that they are available to you in the present and future as they have been in the past. Realize that because this sacred place is in you, you can never really be helpless.

Let yourself remember that as a creature of the universe you receive energy from all the world about you. Feel yourself grounded and feel yourself receiving strength from the center of the earth.

See yourself walking among choices. Remember that you may say yes to those that fit you and gently turn away from those that do not. Give yourself the affirmation "I am able to choose what is good for me."

Breathe deeply and, when you are ready, open your eyes.

The ancient literature of the Aztecs contains this brief verse:

It's springtime.
The Giver of life
    descends in songs attired:
As do leaves
    dressed in fresh young flowers.
From within your Soul come forth,
    to our existence, intoxicating blossoms.

These words eloquently express a simple truth: when we open ourselves to the enormous treasures that surround us, the giver of life visits our being, and we respond from within our soul with intoxicating, beautiful, indescribable internal changes. We blossom from within. Our mind and body react with health and productivity and healing and well-being. We find meaning for life, and we experience overwhelming vitality. We feel at one with the universe, and each of us becomes a pipeline to universal intelligence and wisdom.

Let me return to Jim Hauser, the man whose story

began this chapter. Near the end of his recuperation in his daughter's home, Mr. Hauser related to Mary the following dream: he dreamed he was a passenger on an airplane, sitting at the back of the plane. The plane was flying low over a large city and at times sunk down into the valleys created by the looming skyscrapers. The plane banked and turned in a dangerous but exhilarating manner. It was a beautiful and exciting flight. Mr. Hauser, despite having flown airplanes commercially for thirty-six years, was over-whelmed with fear in his dream. He decided to go up to the cockpit to see who the captain was. When he opened the door to the captain's cabin, he was surprised and pleased to find that the captain was his deceased older brother, Gray, whom he had loved and admired all his life.

Seeing him standing there in the doorway, his brother said, "Jim, you go back to your seat and relax. I'll fly this flight for you."

Each of us is the recipient of everything that has gone before us. We have access to all of human experience, to all of our older "brothers and sisters" who have gone before us. They are there to lead and encourage and inspire us. We have vast resources at our disposal, from which we may freely draw. We, like Jim Hauser, can relax and enjoy the flight.

Chapter 6

❖

How We Block Ourselves from Joy

When I stopped resisting, when I stopped trying to change, when I trusted that there was nothing missing inside, that I didn't have to choose between one part of me over another, I rediscovered me.

—Sue Bender

❖ Benedicta Ward, in her book *The Sayings of the Desert Fathers*, tells about a visit of Abba Lot to Abba Joseph. A devout man who methodically did what was required of him, Abba Lot was interested in deepening his spiritual life. He listed for Abba Joseph all the things he did: "As far as I can I say my little office, I fast a little, I pray and meditate, I live in peace, and as far as I can, I purify my thoughts. What else can I do?" The old man stood up and stretched forth his hands. "If you will," he responded fervently, "you can become all flame."

Why is it that we have such resistance to passionate living? Why do we resist the things that bring us real life and joyful living and fill our lives with that which brings only dissatisfaction? If our inner being is so beautiful, and if by living from that center we can have life at its fullest, why isn't everyone eager to do it? If risk and challenge are so fantastic, why do we build such strong defenses and become so skilled at playing it safe? If our soul is so rich and fulfilling, why do we live so much of our lives as if it did not exist?

I often ask my undergraduate students, "How many of you can draw?" In a class of fifty or so, only three or four raise their hands. Then I ask, "How many would have raised your hands if I had asked you that question when you were in kindergarten?" Most everybody raises their hands to this question. "What happened to you," I ask in mock surprise, "between the age of five and now?"

Something terribly negative comes over us during those years. It takes the "fire" out of us. We close down and lose sight of our capabilities. We start to see the expectations of others and lose the ability to see our own pictures. As a result, our efforts at artful self-expression degenerate into a wooden attempt to put on the page what we think others expect rather than what we see. We do not draw the pictures that dance in our heads but instead try to draw what we think they *should* look like. These attempts to conform freeze us and sap our confidence. Because we resist our inner sight, our creativity vanishes. We do not draw, we write no poetry, we dance little, and we sing few songs because we reject our own inner being. Real art of any type demands letting go and trusting. It is the expression of inner discernment. When we lose that vision, we send away a large chunk of ourselves.

We replace our lost parts with second-best. Alan Jones confesses in his wonderful book on personhood, *Soul Making*, that he often is satisfied with second-best because he is afraid of what would happen to him if he actually discovered the potential within. He borrows from C. S. Lewis's *Surprised by Joy*, in which Lewis defines joy as "an unsatisfied desire which is itself more desirable than any other satisfaction." Jones comments on this definition: "What I find disturbing is my fear of this joy, my terror at the thought of being possessed by real desire. *That is why I would often prefer to make do with second best* [italics added]. Surely my desire would consume me?"

Hildegarde of Bingen was a Christian mystic of the Middle Ages. She described the coming of the fire into her life when she was forty-two years old: a "light of great flashing poured down from the open sky, setting on fire my entire head, all my breast and my whole heart." From that time, Hildegarde found herself possessed of a great insight into life. She decided to try writing and, receiving strength to rise from her sickbed, spent the remaining ten years of her life producing an amazing body of spiritual literature. The Catholic priest, Matthew Fox, claims on the basis of these writings that she was one of the most remarkable persons of Western civilization.

Ernest Holmes portrays this same passionate confidence when he relates the story of his visit to a young woman who was a songwriter. After she played a new tune for him on the piano, he responded, "That's sweet. Are there any words?" "Yes," she replied, "but I don't know what they are." Then she continued, "Someday I'll play this over and as I play it the words will be there."

Letting Down the Nets

According to John's gospel, there was a time when the disciples grew discouraged with Jesus and abandoned him. Nothing, it seemed, was to come of this venture, and in a spirit of pragmatic self-interest they gave up on him and took off. Reverting to their old ways, they climbed aboard their fishing boats and returned to their former lives.

As luck would have it, they fished the night through,

and their toil came to nothing. Just as dawn broke Jesus stood, unrecognized, on the shore and admonished them: "Let down your nets on the starboard side, and you will make a catch." For some unknown reason, they followed the advice of the shadowy stranger on the shore and let the nets down into the water that had recently produced so little. This time, however, the catch was so great they could not haul it into the boat.

THE DARK VOID   This simple story reminds us of two important things that we must do in order to open ourselves again to the richness of our own interior life. First, we have to enter the dark void. The waters of that area of our being are dark and forbidding to us. Our souls are, to say the least, uncharted territory. We are creatures of the dry land, unfamiliar with the deep waters of our being. Like the disciples, we have, or so we thought, fished those waters and come up empty-handed. We now believe that they can yield nothing that we need or want.

Yet, everything is there. Alfred Romer reminds us that we have no alternative to entering this void. He says that the darkness is "pure terror" and that to turn downward into it is to know that "there is no God." Paradoxically, we do not face this darkness in order to return purified to find God. Rather, Romer avers, when "the darkness is upon you, . . . there is God Himself, for God is the greatest destroyer of gods."

If we are ever to go beyond the self-induced illusions that block us from the truth about ourselves, if we are to ever find the foundation of our being and the beginning of reality, we must let our nets descend into that terrible darkness. The truth is that the "catch" is available there and only there.

THE RECEIVING   The second important thing that this simple story teaches us is that our job is to do no more than receive. All that is required of us is to let the nets down.

To do so, we must believe that there are fish there, that we can catch them, and that catching them is worth the effort. We must come to the water on its own terms, ready to seize what it holds for us. The only imperative is to relinquish both resistance and control and simply receive. We create neither the water nor the fish.

Lao Tzu describes the wise man as the one who can receive:

> Without inflaming himself
> He is kindled,
> Without explaining himself
> Is explained,
> Without taking credit
> Is accredited,
> Laying no claim
> Is acclaimed,
> And, because he does not compete,
> Finds peaceful competence.

Foolish persons try to imitate real passion by pretending to inflame themselves, are constantly explaining and justifying themselves, perpetually seek credit and a positive image by placing form over substance, and never find relief from comparing themselves to others. They are constantly in action, but they never receive. Their activities, by which they hope to bring life and joy into their existences, are in reality defenses against life. They resist the very thing they seek.

RESISTANCE TECHNIQUES So what stops us from venturing into those waters? Each of us has a number of "resistance techniques" that we use to keep our nets in the boat.

- FEAR. We fear the unknown, having to change, what we might discover in those deep waters, and the evil we imagine might be unleashed from those waters. We are afraid that other people will see us as different or weird.

Fear makes us worry, and worry forces us into control. We try to control what might happen to us in the future. We must control what people think of us. We must ward off anything we anticipate as painful or that will cause us to struggle. It is a vicious cycle: we worry about what we fear; we try to control what we worry about; we fear what we think we must control.

- SEEKING A QUICK FIX. We have accepted delivery of a load of garbage. The garbage is the notion that success measured in dollars and cents produces the good life. The idea that happiness is an inside job feels strange to us. New ways of thinking demand new ways of behavior. We give up the old only with greatest resistance. It takes time and hard work and patience to learn the new way. We are thin in all these areas, and often we are simply too lukewarm or indifferent to stick with it.

- HEDONISM. Our society places emphasis on hedonistic pleasure as the basis of joy. The expression of our sensuality with as much variety and as often as possible is the most commonly cited recipe for real living. We adhere to the "grab all the gusto you can" and "you only go 'round once" philosophies. We spurn questions of integrity, justice, growth, and interior quality as elements of a repressive past.

- UNAWARENESS. Many people, perhaps most, live their lives as if the inner life did not exist. It is as if they are looking the other way and fail to see it. Others know about it, maybe talk about it, but don't know it.

- DEVALUING OURSELVES. Many people think that they do not deserve it or that they are not good enough. They hear a voice that tells them, "Others may get this, but you never will. You are not ready yet. *You* are not enough."

- OVEREMPHASIS ON ACTIVITY AND PRODUCTIVITY. Our society honors activism and scorns introspection. The quiet way, so necessary to achieve these new goals, is considered a waste of time. Some consider these activities selfish narcissism and self-centeredness. We become so busy that there is no time or energy for these things.
- DISCOUNTING FEELINGS. We develop mechanisms designed to help us avoid feelings. For example, anger is an emotion that makes us uncomfortable, and we will try anything to keep ourselves and others unaware of it. We push ourselves to live up to unrealistic expectations and, consequently, leave our anger unresolved. Buried out of sight, but not out of mind, the anger grows and actually produces more anger. Finally, we *depress* all feelings. When we reach this stage, little of anything feels good, and nothing motivates. Feeling tired, we visit our physician, who prescribes an antidepressant that further removes us from our feelings.

Steve is a person who illustrates most of these resistance techniques. He is a client with whom I have worked for about a year. Steve is a handsome and physically fit forty-five-year-old who takes care of his body with proper nutrition and exercise. He and his intelligent and beautiful wife have two sons and a daughter. All three children are grown and gone from home. Steve says that he has a "close family," but "enmeshed" is perhaps a better way to describe his family. His wife is very religious and requires all other family members to be observant as she is. His children are still financially dependent on him and their mother. Appearances are the most important consideration in decisions about what the family is allowed to do. They all constantly ask, "What will others think if I do such and such?" Everybody keeps many secrets in this family.

The family in which Steve grew up was unusually successful in material terms. His father amassed a fortune in the oil business. Steve and his only brother followed the father's model, and his brother made it. Steve didn't. He made some bad investments, one thing led to another, and he went broke. Now he lives on a family trust, and the interest from his joint ventures with his "wiser" and "successful" brother. He sees himself as a failure and still pushes himself to live up to the perfectionistic standards that have driven his father and brother and that he is passing on to his own children. He is depressed.

Steve told me one day that he wishes he could be a high school teacher. "What stops you?" I asked. His eyes grew big with sadness and brimmed with tears that he could not cry as he whispered, "I could never tell my father that I was going to be a teacher. He wouldn't understand, and he would never approve."

Steve is angry. But because he is "religious," as defined by his wife, he cannot deal with the anger. He must pretend that he is not angry, and consequently he carries around a wagonload of unresolved anger in his unconscious. Some of it goes all the way back to his childhood. Steve is angry with his parents, his brother, his wife, his children, his church, God, and himself. And all this anger sits there in his deep unconscious, rotting away like a cancer. His physician has prescribed a powerful antidepressant, which he has taken daily for almost four years and fears giving up.

Steve's life is permeated by devices that deny him his birthright of peace and love and joy. He is but a shadow of what he was created to be. If he is to find healing, he must let down the nets into these dark, forbidding waters and bring to the light of day all the material that is sapping the life out of him.

So far he cannot. He refuses to question his religion, to

question the rules and expectations with which he grew up, to question his wife, to look at his own unreasonable perfectionism, to question the standards of success with which he has measured himself and other men. He is afraid; he worries. He avoids the feelings and holds on to the old habits. He continues to do the things he has always done and to get the things he always got. He cannot bear the thought of the changes that would take place if he let his nets down. They stay safely and neatly tucked away in his airtight boat. And the catch avoids him.

THE TECHNIQUE OF NONRESISTANCE

The opposite of resistance is nonresistance, a principle with which we are all too unfamiliar. Nonresistance is the physical principle by which the seed, having fallen in the soft and moist earth, opens itself up to the life that is within.

It is this type of nonresistance to which Wu Ming Fu, a Chinese poet and philosopher, calls us in our human existence:

> The seed that is to grow
> must lose itself as seed;
> And they that creep
> may graduate through
> chrysalis to wings.
>
> Wilt thou then, O mortal,
> cling to husks which
> falsely seem to you
> the self?

Actually, the principle of nonresistance is available to us in many ways of which we are unaware. Take sunrise as an example: I love the early morning and watch the sun rise most every day. I stand in my back yard among the trees and bushes and plants with which I share life. The fog shrouds my pasture, and in the distance large trees and small hills form a silhouette against which the morning breaks. The occasional distant dog's bark or the soft call of a bird are the only sounds that disturb my reverie. My posture is a prayer as, in worshipful gratitude, I witness the beautiful spreading of the pink and orange and red of the coming day. I remind myself that I neither create nor control any of it. I am a bystander and an onlooker in the most literal sense. I create neither the light nor the dark it displaces. I only receive: I do not control or direct. Day comes as a gift to warm the land and germinate the seeds and ripen the fruit and provide the light in which we do our work.

I could, of course, resist the day by turning my back to it or closing my eyes or pretending that it is still night. I think that is what Thoreau had in mind when he said, "Only that day dawns to which we are awake." But my resistance would do no more than block my experience of the reality. The sun would not fall from the sky just because I refused to see it.

I like the word *acquiescence* to describe the concept of nonresistance. It comes from a Latin root that means to be at rest. The dictionary says that when we acquiesce, we accept, comply, or consent quietly without protest. The acquiescing person, then, yields, or receives, with quiet submission. So does the opening bloom, water flowing naturally and without resistance downhill, and the squirrel stowing away his winter's stock of nuts. Each in its own way submits without protest to the laws that govern its nature. There is no resistance. In her book, *Every Bush Is Burning*, Joan Puls reports that once, while watching a seagull fly, she remembered the line from Joan Cox: "Freedom is complete obedience to the element for which we were designed."

What Resistance Costs Us

Betsy Caprio and Thomas Hedberg, in their book *Coming Home,* cite an anonymous individual who says, "What I've learned is that my insides respond to the way I treat them —that's not a very good way to put it, but I think you know what I mean." I think this wise person is saying that there are consequences associated with how we treat our interior being, our insides. We speak about "gut feelings" and about things that are "heartfelt." We ask, "Do you have the stomach for it?" and refer to ourselves and others as "heartsick." We refer to a "lump in the throat" and describe certain things as "heartbreaking" or "hard to stomach." Other things, we say, are a "pain in the neck." These and many other phrases give evidence to the truth that what we feel and what is occurring in our lives have an impact on our bodies. We cannot ignore our gut or heart or one side of our brain without peril.

All this means that the techniques we develop to resist opening up to our inner reality have consequences. These consequences may be divided into three levels.

LEVEL ONE   At this level we believe that our feelings are not okay, that we must hide them from others. We "stuff" or "hold in" feelings. At first, we are comfortable being aware of these feelings, but we do not want others to know about them. Eventually, we begin to deny our feelings even to ourselves. A very narrow spectrum of feelings is deemed to be appropriate, and we try to keep ourselves within these emotional boundaries. We deny any feelings outside these narrow parameters and hide them from others.

This technique is often described as "pushing our feelings down" because what we do is push the feelings into our unconscious. It is as if we keep a large garbage can beneath the surface of our conscious mind and stuff our unwanted feelings and unwanted parts of ourselves into that pail. These feelings and parts of our being do not disappear, however. They remain real and present even though they are unrecognized and unresolved. Unfortunately, as far as feelings are concerned, getting something out of sight in no way enables us to avoid the consequences. On the contrary, the longer the feelings are suppressed, the greater the consequences grow. Our subterranean feelings continue to affect our thinking and behavior, even though we may have them conveniently out of our conscious mind.

Here are some of the specific ways we push our feelings down:

- *Denying that they are there.* That is, we refuse to give them conscious acknowledgment.
- *Substituting one feeling for another.* For example, because anger is considered a negative emotion, we substitute anxiety for it.
- *Finding positive names for self-destructive behaviors.* For example, we justify avoiding confrontation because we "do not want to hurt him." Or, we label dealing directly with our needs "selfishness" and call denying them "love."
- *Making emotions physical by getting sick.* We get headaches, backaches, insomnia, or ulcers or develop any one of an endless list of other physical problems.
- *Worrying.* Instead of taking action and facing our fears, we picture the worst and worry about it. When we do, our imagination, our greatest potential for joy, becomes our greatest enemy.
- *Overeating, oversleeping, taking drugs, or engaging in some other addictive activity.*
- *Becoming passive-aggressive.* That is, we take our emotions out on people in indirect ways.
- *Suppressing our feelings.* We turn all our emotions inward on ourselves and refuse to feel anything.

- *Overworking.*
- *Trying harder to get it right.*

LEVEL TWO   At this level, the feelings that we have tried to stuff away into the unwanted and unknown parts of ourselves begin to squeeze out through the cracks. They emerge as unhealthy and destructive forces.

We may begin to have anxiety attacks or to engage in avoidance tactics such as projecting on others the characteristics we hate in ourselves. We may strike out in blind rage or by battering the helpless—children, the elderly, or anyone else who is weaker than we are. We may allow ourselves to be victimized by remaining in relationships where we are emotionally or physically abused. Our eating habits may degenerate into bulimia, anorexia, or compulsive overeating. We may become a workaholic and lose ourselves in our vocations. We may become obsessed with our sexuality and act out sexually.

Level Two is the point in our lives at which we begin to fall apart. The emotional and physical consequences of resisting our inner reality shows up in our daily behaviors. The symptoms, over which we have no control, become apparent to others, and these patterns begin to disturb our relationships.

LEVEL THREE   At this level the resistance techniques become overwhelming and are most destructive. What began as coping mechanisms that enabled us to survive become, at this extreme, totally disabling symptoms.

Full-blown emotional disorders such as paranoia, schizophrenia, and manic-depression may appear. Individuals may develop life-styles that are self-mutilating, such as substance abuse and suicidal ideation. We may develop a terminal illness. Or, some of us may turn to sexual perversions such as various forms of sexual addiction, pedophilia, rape, or other sexual violence.

Figuring Out Where We Are

How can we tell that life isn't much fun anymore? That may seem like a silly question at first. The truth is that we become so adept at our resistance techniques and so entrenched in the ruts of life that we lose sight of what is really going on in our lives. We don't know what is normal and have no real benchmarks to determine what is happening within us. We lose confidence in knowing what we really want. In fact, the resistance techniques are *designed* to keep us from knowing the truth about ourselves. Something must intervene to wake us up.

LOOKING FOR LOVE IN ALL THE WRONG PLACES In *Another Chance* Sharon Wegscheider-Cruse describes our disturbing ability to lose our way while seeking beneficial goals. She tells us that so much of the struggle of life comes not because "people intentionally escape into sick or painful behavior" but because people are trying to find what they genuinely need for life. They are "looking for a flow into life not an escape from it." But, she maintains, "A troubled person often is a seeker for a full life who does not know how to seek."

In our effort to find the full life, we get shunted onto pathways that are dead ends. The simple truth about the majority of us is that we are searching for a "flow into life." We want experiences that are full and meaningful. But we get into trouble because we lose the way and do not even realize that we are lost. And the more lost we are, generally, the more frantic, even desperate, we get in our effort to achieve the good life.

In the words of a popular country and western song, we "look for love in all the wrong places." I have witnessed people searching for life by following dead-end paths. And

I have myself tried to find love and fulfillment in all the wrong places myself. Here are a few of our dead-end pathways:

1. Security. We seem to think that we can find a place where we will not be vulnerable. We build walls in order to remove risk from our lives. We try to hide the truth from ourselves and others.

2. Love from someone else. We believe that if we can be tolerable to other people, we will somehow be acceptable. Our motto is "If only so-and-so will love me, I will be okay."

3. Success and prestige. We think that if we have the trappings of material prosperity and accomplishment, then other people will look up to us and we will be okay. We really do think that money will buy happiness.

4. A painless, trouble-free life. Peace of mind, as defined from this perspective, is to have no problems. Our belief is that if we can get to this point, life will be great.

5. Control and power over others. If we can obtain power and make other people do what we want when we want it, then we will be okay.

6. Food, drugs, work, money, or praise.

What do you seek that cannot really bring you wholeness and happiness in life? Can you add to this list? Please write your answers below.

WARNING SIGNS   Certain warning signs can alert us that we are denying our inner reality. There are symp-

toms we can look for that reveal that we are blocking ourselves from the joy, love, and peace we deserve and are
seeking. We can determine whether or not we are in trouble.

The following statements serve as a "HOW AM I DOING
WITH MY LIFE?" test. Please respond to them with a TRUE or a
FALSE according to what you think is true about you in an
overall sense. Consider each statement, and the test as a
whole, as a method of discerning trends or patterns in your
life.

1. I am uncomfortable with people I consider my
   equals or my superiors.
2. It's harder for me to get up and go to work than it
   used to be.
3. I am easily hurt.
4. I suspect the intentions of other people.
5. I reject others.
6. I sometimes wish I were someone else.
7. I am often irritable and must work hard to control
   my anger.
8. I find it difficult to believe that others like and/or
   love me.
9. I seldom approve of the way I do my job.
10. Most of the time, I feel unsuccessful in my career.
11. I demand perfection of myself.
12. I am constantly driven to "do better."
13. I find it difficult to relax and do nothing.
14. I am tired most of the time.
15. I have difficulty getting started on projects I am
    afraid I cannot do well.
16. I have a great fear of failure.
17. I seldom ask directly for what I want.
18. I often wonder if I am in the right line of work.
19. Playing isn't much fun for me anymore.
20. Most of the time I do not like my life.

If you responded TRUE to eight or more of these questions, it is time to consider what is going on in your life.

THE EMOTIONAL SURVIVAL PACK Let's pretend that you are to be shipwrecked on an emotional island with one hundred other people and that you can only take five things for your emotional survival and mental health. Let's say, further, that these five things must be inner abilities or talents, not external objects. That is, they must be characteristics or attributes that belong to your personality or character. They may not be physical articles. What would you take?

Consider some of the following items:

- The ability to like and respect myself
- The ability to make and save money
- The ability to take responsibility for myself, grow as a person, and take risks
- Physical beauty
- The ability to compare myself to others
- The ability to look young
- The ability to love and accept others without the need to control them
- The ability to feel insecure and uncertain on important occasions
- Faith and spirituality
- My sexually seductive powers
- The ability to know my wants and to nurture myself
- Leadership qualities
- The ability to get attention
- The ability to experience feelings and express them appropriately
- My family name
- The ability to impress and manipulate other people
- The ability to be depressed, consumed with fear, and co-dependent
- My prestige and status in the community

Please write out the things you would take. You may include anything on the list that you wish.

After each quality, write out briefly how it would help you survive emotionally and keep you mentally healthy.

THIRTEEN PROVEN METHODS TO KEEP JOY OUT OF YOUR LIFE   Finally, consider the following methods of deflecting joy from your life. How many of these are you guilty of? Are you really good at any of them? After looking over the list, contemplate what your overall response means about you and where you need to change.

HOW TO KEEP JOY, PEACE, AND LOVE OUT OF YOUR LIFE

1. Hide your feelings. People are interested in your strengths and don't care about what you feel. Therefore, try never to express your feelings and needs directly and openly, especially with "loved ones."
2. Select one or two people and pattern your life after them completely. Wish to be them rather than yourself.
3. Abstain from experiencing any sense of humor.
4. When things go wrong, blame other people, and always justify yourself. Refuse to admit any weakness, and resist changing anything about yourself.
5. Develop a strong critical side. Find fault in everyone, including yourself.

6. Take no risks, because that way you ensure that you will never flop. Risk only leads to disappointment, failure, and pain. Do only what is easiest, and always play it safe. It's okay to talk about risk, but never get involved in things. Procrastinate.
7. Never listen to your body. Rather, use it and abuse it. Fill it with junk foods and drugs. Do not exercise. Get too much sleep sometimes, and then don't get enough. Never have a sense of gratitude and appreciation for what your body does for you and others. Hate your body.
8. Never cry. If you do, never let anyone see you.
9. Never talk about your problems, and never reveal your weaknesses. Try to keep them from even yourself.
10. Always expect the worst. Saturate your mind with negative images. Expect yourself and others to let you down. Never trust. Tell yourself that you are being realistic.
11. Shun even the appearance of intimacy. Do not let anyone get close to you, and never need anything from anyone. To do so only makes you vulnerable and will make you weak.
12. Remember that success in life is always material gain and that, as the bumper sticker says, "Whoever has the most toys when he dies, wins."
13. Forget about spirituality. That stuff is for softies and is not a part of the real world. Remember, you can't pay the rent or buy groceries with prayer and meditation!

One of my students, Stephanie Helms, wrote the following poem as part of a class assignment in which she described her childhood. The poem was modeled on Walt Whitman's classic, "There Was a Child Went Forth." This twenty-two-year-old woman elegantly described the things she had seen as a child that had become a part of her:

There was a child went forth every day,
And the first object she looked upon,
    that object she became.
The smell of sweet honeysuckle
Angry, loud words,
a slap.
A light under the door,
    he's coming,
    shattered dishes,
    broken glass.
Hate.
Fear.
    a blackened eye,
    bruises.
How could she have said those things?
How could he have done those things?
    self-blame,
    self-hate,
    "It's all my fault."
The cold, loving nose of a dog,
    my dog.
Death.
One more thing I did wrong,
Confusion.
The sweet, scary smell of pot.
Skipping across green grass.
Growing up in a household filled
    with hate.
The air heavy, laden with
    untold secrets.
All of us, my brother, my mom,
    myself
    victims, and yet, abusers.
How could I have hurt him so?
I still feel to blame for his
    childhood.

I should have been better.
Lost,
Wasted time.
Tears,
    too many tears.
Betrayal,
    they knew and yet did nothing.

This poem brought much pain to Stephanie. The events themselves were awful for a little girl, and they were no less traumatic in the recollection. Cruelty, divorce, fear, abondonment, shame, death, betrayal—all these and more were documented in her poem. Why introduce such pain into her life? Wouldn't it be better, as much of our culture encourages, to "let sleeping dogs lie"? Why not forget the past? After all, it *is* past, isn't it? Isn't it better to live in the present? It is tempting to evade the pain and effort of looking squarely at how we got to where we are.

I watched this young woman read this poem to her fifty classmates. Somehow, at the beginning of her adult life, she knows that these things are *not* past. She knows for herself the truth in Faulkner's phrase "There are places one may go in the South where past history is neither past nor is it history." "These events are a part of me," she said, holding back the tears, "and they bring great pain and sadness to the surface as I talk about them. And yet, I am aware that they have shaped my life in positive ways. They have made me strong, more human, and more humanitarian. I understand and care more."

As she talked, I watched silently. I sensed her courage as she forced herself to reveal these things about herself. Then I perceived what I interpreted as a slight change in her. I noted that her tears, which at first swam in her eyes, turned into smiles. To use our metaphor from earlier in this chapter, she dropped her nets into the dark waters. That is the scary part and the part that demands courage. Then, something happened in her. That which was so overwhelmingly powerful in her life lost its strength. She sensed herself from a different perspective. Autobiography, as Frederick Buechner tells us, is not only self-revelation, it is also self-discovery.

I noted a sparkle in Stephanie's eyes when the class was over. I believe that little spark is another step in her becoming "all flame."

Chapter 7

❖

THE SOUL'S PURSUIT OF LIFE

Too often we act as if we were put on this earth to die.

—Ken Macrorie

❖ *June Bug was an old spotted* mare with whom I shared life many years ago. Although she had a foal every spring for several years, I never saw her give birth. She always managed to fool us and make us think the big event was still a few days off. Then, during the night, while no one was there to see or help, she had her baby.

Once I did arrive shortly after the colt was born. He was all legs, like a little stack of crooked sticks with a head and ears, lying there where he had been born. He was wet and slick, and Mama was licking him dry and nosing him in gentle encouragement to stand. It didn't take long. His legs were rickety and unreliable as he tried, several times unsuccessfully, to get to his feet. But then everything worked. Those long legs, unsure and wobbly, unfolded somehow, and the baby pushed himself to his feet. His hind end rose before his front legs could figure it all out. He wove unsteadily, half up and half down, and kept at it. Finally, all four legs were widespread under him, and he stood teetering and swaying as if to say, "Now what do I do?" Mama was never far away. She assisted and encouraged with licks and grunts and nudges.

Then, on legs that were still unreliable, the baby managed a step, moving toward his mother and life, searching for his mother's udder. He looked uncertainly in all the wrong places. He bumped dubiously, but insistently, between her front legs, tenaciously seeking the teat and the life-giving warm milk. Not only was he uncertain where anything was, he did not even know for sure what it was that he was looking for. Yet he persisted, and finally the search paid off. His efforts met with reward: he found the spot and drank.

That colt's instinctive search for the source of life is, to me, a perfect picture of soul-business. In *Man for Himself,* Erich Fromm called it "the life-furthering energy," and we can see it in all living things. We witness it in microscopic seeds that fall into the narrow cracks of concrete and strain through the cement and steel to the moist earth beneath. Acorns sprout in rain gutters on our houses. On the side of a harsh mountain crag, a juniper tree struggles to find nourishment and moisture in the forbidding rock. Most of its lower limbs are lifeless, but at the top are green sprouts and small, round, bluish berries that are seeds of the next generation. A potato, stored in a dark bin under our cabinets, stretches out toward the light with spindly, yellow sprouts in a bizarre and futile effort to grow. No matter how inhospitable the environment, life seeks to thrive. Every living thing strives to mature and fulfill its potential. Even in the most adverse circumstances, nature seeks to heal herself as every living thing reaches out to life in the same way that the colt's hungry mouth searches for its mother's teat.

Deep within each of us is that same hunger. We may

be unaware of it, or we may be so shut down that it becomes virtually ineffective. The reality is that it is there all along, and we can allow our being to be guided by that craving. We can push our real self out of hiding, go beyond our self-protective, fearful defenses, and follow the inner yearning for self-expression. When we do, we are born. We transcend mere existence and become alive. Dag Hammarskjold described his response to that inner urge to life when in *Markings* he wrote,

> I don't know Who—or what—put the question, I don't even remember answering. But at some moment I did answer *Yes* to Someone—or Something—and from that hour I was certain that existence was meaningful and that, therefore, my life, in self-surrender, had a goal.
>
> From that moment I have known what it means "not to look back," and "to take no thought for the morrow."

This incarnational "yes-saying" is a dynamic and ongoing experience. It is like breathing; we stop at our own peril. In that sense, we are born anew each day, and our life is the unfolding and affirmation of the specifics of our inner being. In his book *Man for Himself*, Erich Fromm tells about a late nineteenth-century Japanese artist named Hokusai who at age seventy-five wrote about the developmental evolution of his talent for painting. His passion for art began at age six. By age fifty, he had published an infinity of designs, but, he said, nothing produced before age seventy was worth taking into account. By age seventy-three, he confessed, "I [had] learned a little about the real structure of nature, of animals, plants, birds, fishes and insects." As a result, "when I am eighty, I shall have made more progress; at ninety I shall penetrate the mystery of things; at a hundred I shall certainly have reached a marvelous stage and when I am a hundred and ten, everything I do, be it a dot or a line, will be alive." He signs this testimony "the old man mad about drawing."

When we become alive in this total way, we receive our soul. This is what the Russians mean by the term *zhivaya zhizn,* or "living life," and what the French mean when they speak of *joie de vivre,* or the "joy of life." That is what Lao Tzu meant by the Tao, what Buddha meant by enlightenment, and what Jesus meant by abundant life. It is the joy of the soul.

Chasing a Mirage of Life

Dave is a client of mine who is a college professor. A graduate of one of the best universities in the South, he is at the height of a very successful career in teaching and research. He is fifty years old, is sought as a speaker on environmental issues, is well thought of in his community, and enjoys a positive reputation among his peers. He is a handsome man, with a strong, slim, healthy body. He has a keen mind and money in the bank. Dave's problem is that he is alone. He said to me the other day, "I have played it safe all my life. As a result, my life is empty. I have no close friends; I have no intimate relationships. I don't love anyone, and no one loves me. I thought my work was enough to give me all the love I needed. The truth is, I was afraid of intimacy and didn't believe I could ever have it. I have ended up safe but alone. Now I have nothing, and I'm scared to death that it is too late." Dave wept as he spoke these words.

I know how he felt. My mistakes took another form, but, like Dave, I pursued an illusion. I used up my soul's hunger for life by chasing a mirage. Like a thirsty person in the desert, I thought I was moving toward a cool, blue lake, and when I got there I planned to jump in head-first for a delicious swim in the life-giving water. When I arrived, however, I found only more dry sand and nothing to quench my thirst.

Like the foolish priest in Anthony de Mello's story "The Monster in the River," I had been busy stalking deathly shadows and chasing self-deceptions that I erroneously called life. As de Mello tells it:

> The village priest was distracted in
> his prayers by children playing outside
> his window. To get rid of them
> he shouted, "There's a terrible monster
> down at the river. Hurry there
> and you will see him breathing fire
> through the nostrils."
>
> Soon the whole village had
> heard of this monstrous apparition
> and was rushing to the river.
> When the priest saw this
> he joined the crowd. As he panted
> his way to the river, which was four
> miles away, he thought, "It is true
> I invented the story. Still
> you can never tell!"

Like the priest, I ran panting after phantoms, some of which I had invented myself, in the vain hope that I would find peace and fulfillment and joy for my life. But what I sought in the name of life only took life from me. I looked alive, but I really wasn't. One of my clients recently described her life as "trying to open a lock with the wrong key." I empathized with her.

As I look back across my life, I realize that I have tried many wrong keys. When I examine them, I see that I have tried to unlock life's mysteries with three keys that are illusions: 1) I needed acceptance from other people in order to accept myself; 2) I believed I could find fulfillment in what

I produced; and 3) I thought failure and loss were all I could expect in life because there was some inadequacy in me.

All this came from early training and some accidental events that shaped how I thought about myself and my world. I cannot remember a time in life when I did not fear that I was different from other people and that I was an outsider because of it. For some reason, I thought of myself as less than others and that it was not okay for me to be me. Even in grade school I remember feeling that I didn't really fit in.

Once when I was about seven I told my Sunday School teacher that I had been taking tap-dancing lessons and I was an expert at it. It was a lie. I wanted her and the class to be impressed with me and think I was special. My teacher placed a chair at the front of the class and told me to get up on it and dance. The next thing I knew I was up on that chair with ten or twelve youngsters and my teacher looking up at me. I didn't know the first thing about tap dancing. I could only stand there until she told me to get down. I still remember how fiery-hot my cheeks burned in humiliation as I crawled down from that chair.

Even at that age, I clearly felt that I was unacceptable and that if I wanted to be accepted, I would have to hide my true identity and pretend to be something I was not. I felt, as Ruth Fishel put it, that "there was hardly a time I thought that I wouldn't give life everything that I had. There was certainly a time that I thought that everything I had was not enough." I sensed myself as weird, strange, not really a part of the group. *Lonely* is the most appropriate word to describe my life in those years. These feelings were true at school and church and, especially, at home.

Feelings of being weird and lonely and unacceptable are a frightening experience for a child. Like any other child feeling unacceptable, I confronted a basic question: how do I survive in these circumstances? My answer came in the form of three experiences that became the basis of my illusions.

The first originated from an idle comment made by a man named Chester Gill. I remember him as a kind and generous person who lived in our community and went to our church. He was a farmer and had hired me to do some work for him. I was digging away in his field, and he and my mother were talking. They were almost out of earshot, and I am sure they both thought I could not hear their conversation. But my ears were sharp when other people were discussing me. Mr. Gill said to my mother, "Jimmy is the hardest-working boy I have ever seen." There was admiration in his voice. I can't remember my mother's exact response, but I could tell she was pleased. Mr. Gill's comment made an indelible impression on my soul that day: what I heard was "If you want people to like you, be the hardest worker anyone has ever seen."

I formed my second illusion when I received my first A at school. I had never been a good student, and school was something I merely tolerated for the most part. I loved to learn and had always been intellectually curious, but doing well in school was something that I thought I could not do. Then Mrs. Forrest, my ninth-grade civics teacher, gave me an A for the first six weeks of school. I remember the exact spot in the hall outside her classroom door where I stood staring at the grade. I could not believe it. I was thrilled. Mrs. Forrest gave me my second clue: If you want people to like you, make top grades in school.

The third illusion came at church. I went to church as a kid because my mother took me. I was a very spiritual little boy, and the idea of God and prayer and a world beyond our senses were very appealing to me. Church, however, was something else. We went to a small, rural Protestant church. It was the only church in the community, and all who attended were neighbors. I was enormously bored by the long sermons, the repetitive ceremonies, and the impossibly unimaginative perspectives that were presented to me. Somehow in the midst of these unpleasant circumstances, I heard people say things like "Jimmy is not like other young people." They meant that I was a "good boy," different from other kids, somehow better than normal teenagers. They observed that I did not do the things that other kids did. I never rebelled, I went to church, and I did whatever was the proper thing to do. I was polite to adults and obedient to my teachers. They *liked* the way I was. I found in these sentiments my third tactic for survival: Be more religious, more polite, more passive than anyone has ever imagined a teenager to be.

My life strategy was now set. I knew how to survive in a world that I saw as fundamentally hostile and where I believed it was dangerous to be the me I really was. I had my program for life firmly established by the ripe old age of fourteen. I knew what it took to gain the acceptance that I feared would elude me.

Being Jack and Climbing Beanstalks

My favorite fairy tale has always been "Jack and the Beanstalk." I now know why. This story expresses my philosophy of life and my effort to be a "good boy." It begins with Jack busy, trying to save his unhappy mother from poverty. He gets snookered by a con-man who trades him a few beans for the family cow. Jack plants the beans and soon finds himself having climbed a ropelike bean stalk up to the heavens and sneaking around the house of a giant. Besides trying to keep himself from getting killed, Jack is trying at a fevered pitch to steal the giant's goose, which lays golden eggs. If he can pull it off and make it safely down the beanstalk, he will have financial success and security for the rest of his life. If he can filch the giant's property and kill the giant, he and his mother will live happily ever after. Jack will be a hero.

In the fairy tale, Jack pulls it off. I didn't. The reason

was that my formula was wrong. Here, in a nutshell, were my garbled thoughts: in order to be a part of the group, I must set myself apart from the rest by being different and better than anyone else. Be the hardest worker anyone ever saw. Make the top grades and be the best boy that has ever lived.

I clung to this mind-set with a vengeance. The beans for which I traded the family cow was the naive belief that I can obtain a positive sense of self-worth from the evaluation of others. That original mistake externalized my value and made me dependent on others for self-respect. I was okay only if *they* saw me as okay.

I was set up for failure because the formula I followed was faulty itself. No matter what I did, what behaviors and thinking and feelings I plugged in, the outcome was always wrong. The inevitable result was that I lost myself, and I also lost any possibility of relationships with others.

Not long ago, I met a man at a workshop who demonstrates the deficiency of my old way of thinking. A fifty-seven-year-old professional, he had all the trappings of a successful man of the nineties. He was well respected in his community, he had a long-standing marriage, and his children all were grown and established in successful careers. He was handsomely dressed, educated, articulate, poised, and self-confident. After several hours of sharing with other men and women, he said, "I spent my life trying to be a success. In that process, I developed a marriage of silence, I lost my sons and they lost me, and I sacrificed my self-respect. And," he paused a moment and then continued with deep sadness in his voice, "I wasn't all that successful anyway."

I knew what he meant, because I had carried the cross he described until I was in my midthirties. Still trying to please, I was filled with a deep-seated anger that emerged as passive-aggression and depression when life unraveled on me. I related in the first chapter of this book the details of what happened. I was living what James Kavanaugh described in *Laughing Down Lonely Canyons*: "We close our eyes and ears to shut out pain, numb our senses to endure the tedious day and unfriendly night, and cling to whatever or whomever is at hand to save us. We work harder, read more, turn to magic or illusion, sex or power or money. *We no longer turn to ourselves* or to others where real strength and love are possible" (emphasis added).

At first glance, Kavanaugh's words are strange. His poems directly address the inadequacy of our modern definitions of life and the values we use to guide ourselves. He writes about how confused and hurt we are, how our culture has savaged us, and how we have lost connection with ourselves, others, and God. Why would he encourage us to turn to ourselves to find deeper, more healthy values for life? Because, I think, he knows that our delusion is that we still think we can find our value outside ourselves: in performance, in work, in sex, in power, in money, in others.

Why must we turn to ourselves? Because inside us is an inner fire that still burns. It is the hunger for life and fulfillment as persons with which we came into this world. It is within us; we possess it already. We turn to ourselves in the same way that a mustard seed turns to itself for the tree it becomes. The tree is there already, within the tiny seed. What is required is no more than simply letting it *become*. The Upanishads, sacred literature of ancient Hinduism, says, "What is within us is also without. What is without is also within."

The Chinese philosopher had that in mind when he said, "What you seek, you already possess." Jesus emphasized this truth when he said, "The kingdom of God is within you." Ralph Waldo Emerson was talking about the same thing when he reminded us that "Tho' we travel the world over to find the beautiful, / We must carry it with us or we find it not."

Moving on from Illusion

Then I discovered me. I began the journey toward what Lao Tzu described as "the wise man." He said that this man, the man of wisdom, relaxes with peaceful competence because he does not strain to take credit, does not live life comparing and competing, and makes no false claims about himself. He is self-contained and, as such, is joyful both inside and out.

I found my soul. I gave unconditional acceptance to me and my life and where I was and where I was going. What I had so long and futilely sought from others, I gave to myself. And freedom came—slowly and not all at once, but it came.

I changed the inner program. I rethought those early messages. I realized how fruitless my efforts had been. Not only were they not effective, they were counterproductive: they got me the exact opposite of what I intended. I sought acceptance, and yet my goal was to be better than anyone else. I wanted to be seen as better than the others, and that objective in itself was enough to *set me apart*. No wonder I felt lonely and left out—I had excluded myself from the group.

I had to learn some new behaviors, thinking, and attitudes. I had to establish contact. I had to learn to sit in the audience and make small talk rather than always be the person in charge. I had to realize that life is a process rather then specific outcomes, no matter how desirable they might be to me. I had to give up controlling other people, and I had to give myself respect regardless of what other people might or might not think. And, most of all, I had to know that none of this would happen overnight.

Let me give what may appear to be an overly simplistic example. I began to attend a men's group at an Episcopal church. There were about a dozen men, including the parish priest, who met together for spiritual growth one Saturday a month. We cooked our breakfast, everyone pitching in. Then we ate. During this process we talked: baseball, flowers, politics, community and church gossip. Then we went into the chapel and celebrated the Eucharist. After that, we went home. I was disappointed. "Nothing happened," I complained to a Jesuit priest friend of mine. "No one taught us anything. We just talked and ate and went home. We did nothing spiritual. I don't think I will go back!"

What I wanted was a program, a controlled presentation that provided me and others with a script. My friend, wiser than I, knew how many things just "happen" in an uncontrolled setting. He responded, "Jim, you need to learn just to be with men. Great things do not have to happen for great things to happen. Go back."

I learned that if I was to discover my soul and possess my life fully, I had to open up to life. I had to take chances by giving up some of the defenses that I had erected to protect myself from being found unacceptable by others. I had to risk "death."

The Illusion of Death

Most of us believe that we want life. Do we, really? Or, is our goal simply not to die? Don't we design our lives to insulate ourselves from anything that might threaten what we believe is safe. If so, our primary objective is survival, safety, continuance, duration, and permanence. Life becomes merely the process of not dying. We become afraid of life because life may lead to death. Thus, because we are afraid to die we become afraid to live.

One of the great illusions we perpetuate is that death will end our lives. But death is not the antitheses of life. It is not even the enemy of life. Death is an integral part of life, just like breathing and eating and thinking.

The antithesis of life, its opposite and great enemy, is mere existence. When we merely exist, we are not fully alive; we only appear to be. We are essentially unliving persons eating and drinking and having sex and making money and praying and wishing. We are inanimate bodies that play the roles of the living. We are like shadows on the nighttime ceiling of a child's bedroom, real only in the mind of the child.

In his wonderful essay entitled "Why the Novel Matters," D. H. Lawrence states that mere existence is "like a pianoforte with half of the notes mute." It is, he continues, "walking around dead and a carcass in the street and house." Living death is the antithesis of life and is the thing that we really have to fear.

Living only to avoid death wipes out life. We do things that we hope will keep pain at bay, cover up our guilt, quiet our fear, or hide our shame. We do not want to fall behind others, have less status than they have, win less respect than our peers, or fail in the eyes of others; so we are busy looking alive. But we are only existing.

At the end of the eighteenth century, Conte Vittorio Alfeiri said, "Often the test of courage is not to die but to live." Later, Robert Cody expressed the same idea: "Have courage to live. Anyone can die."

The challenge, then, is to be alive, to pursue life as the colt pursued its mother's milk. It is to find the hunger and allow it to guide us. That is by no means an automatic process for us. The experiences of life sometimes funnel us into ruts of thinking and feeling that deny the soul's hunger for life. One person said to me as we talked about these issues, "I don't believe I have a hunger for life. I don't even believe I deserve it. I work hard, and I don't ever get what I want. What I do now is just cope with life. I expect bad things to happen, and I try to be ready for them. If you want me to believe in a hunger for real living in me, you have to convince me." Like this person, we can get so far from our soul-hunger that we do not recognize it when it occurs.

Separating the Real from the Fake

Human beings are actually very good at chasing illusions. In fact, we prefer them to reality. Thus, we seek most any method of denying the highest and best of our soul, even from ourselves. In the epilogue of his excellent book *Recovering the Soul,* Larry Dossey clearly describes our efforts to hide the truth about ourselves from ourselves. We are blind, he says, and our whole culture conspires to compound that blindness. Our religious traditions drive home the message that we are despicable, unworthy creatures with no redeemable qualities of our own. When, as has happened frequently in history, individuals arise who clearly sense their inner divinity, they are charged with heresy and blasphemy and are treated inhumanely or killed. Dossey concludes, "These woeful facts reveal the unbelievable lengths to which we will go to hide from our true nature."

Once when I was about sixteen, I woke up in the middle of the night to hear my thirteen-year-old sister crying in the next room. She was moaning with deep sobs that racked her whole body. My parents were in the room with her. Through her tears, I heard her tell of her fear that she had committed the "unpardonable sin." Our minister had preached a sermon earlier that evening on that subject. With the terrifying authority that only a rural southern Protestant minister can evoke, he described in powerful detail the "irrefutable" truth that it's possible to commit a sin that God will never forgive. Hell awaits the wretched creature who does so. My little sister, innocent, lovely, and pure, fell into the pit his words had dug, and her adolescent heart was broken with fear that she had committed that sin. I listened as my father reassured her with soft, comforting words; finally she fell asleep. I have often wondered, in the years since, how deep are the scars left in her life by that event. That, I think, is what Dossey is talking about; and I think he is correct in his conclusion that our culture, through the communication of such concepts, drives us to chase illusions that deny the soul's pursuit of life.

How can we even begin to separate the real from the fake? How may we know if we are hungry for life or if we are doing no more than pursuing our illusions? How can we recognize the soul's hunger for life?

SOUL-HUNGER IS BASED ON A SENSE OF DISEQUILIBRIUM
A sense of personal incompleteness supports the hunger for life that emerges from the soul. When I speak of "incompleteness," I am not referring to the kind of inadequacy or shame that is based on the belief that we are not good enough. John Bradshaw calls that kind of incompleteness "soul-murder."

Rather, soul-hunger is an emptiness, an incompleteness, an inner state of dissatisfaction. It, like physical hunger, pushes us to do something to remove the uncomfortable sense of disquiet within. We want to act in accordance with goals that arise from the heart.

I see this sense of incompleteness in the work of a select number of my students, through their hunger for knowledge and their spiritual quest to grow by exploring new concepts. I see it in their idealism, which makes them believe that their life can make a difference in the world. I see it in their fierce willingness to try new things and stretch themselves.

A client of mine who is an elementary school teacher told me not long ago that she had begun training to become a foster mother. She detailed all the things she could do for foster children and what she hoped to accomplish for them. When I asked her what she wanted to gain for herself, she said simply, "I want to expand my horizons." Her awareness that there were other areas of life where she could grow exemplifies the incompleteness that comes from the soul.

SOUL-HUNGER IS A PASSION In order to talk about the soul's hot pursuit of life, we must talk about love. There is passion involved in soul-hunger. We want to do things beyond just satisfying our basic need to contribute and be creative or useful. We want to make a difference, and the inner drive is based on that need. In the Old Testament, Jeremiah described this dissatisfaction as "the fire in our bones." In *The Power of Myth,* Joseph Campbell called it "following our bliss." We may call it fulfilling our dreams, or acting according to our higher self. Whatever the phrase used to describe it, it is a need to act that emerges from the deep inner recesses of our being. We cannot *not* act on it.

I have seen people who have lost the passion for life. They have been so buffeted about by the things they experience along the way that their soul shrivels up and hides. All kinds of mental and physical disorders emerge when the soul's passion for life is lost. Some people find a way to die. Others strike back at life with cruelty and abuse. Most people simply hunker down and cope. They live what Thoreau described as "lives of quiet desperation."

Those who identify the fire in their bones and allow it to guide them find their expression in a variety of activities. Sometimes it is a desire for learning. Other times it is a love of nature. Or, it may reveal itself as the need to help others. For some it may be music, for others writing. Some of us express it through our jobs, hobbies, or spiritual endeavors. For some it is expressed in vigorous physical activity, and for others it involves quiet repose. Some people require a group of like-minded persons to express their passion, whereas others need complete solitude. The point is that when the passion of the soul expresses itself, it does so in a personal and subjective way. All that is required is that our passion correspond to the deep inner needs of our life.

SOUL-HUNGER IS COMMITMENT Sometimes the word *commitment* is used as if it were synonymous with prison. Commitment, from this perspective, is entrapment. It means that once involved, we can never let go, and thus being committed to something or someone is like putting your foot in a bear trap or being thrown into a dungeon.

To the contrary, instead of seeming like a pit from which there is no escape, commitment is based on trust. To commit implies the delivery of a person or a thing into the charge or care of another in the spirit of mutual trust and openness. One's trust is placed in the assumption that the thing delivered will find safekeeping in the hands of the other. There is never a locked gate in commitment because locks are the antithesis of trust, and where trust is absent commitment can never be.

Thus, when I commit myself to a cause or a person, I *entrust* myself. I want to give my best, and I want long-term involvement. Temporary flashes and halfhearted attempts can never express the deepest needs of our lives. Commitment goes all the way. It sticks. It is faithful and devoted. To do less reveals something less than passionate involvement.

There have been times in my life when I was involved in something to which I was not fully committed. For example, when I was in high school, I got a part-time job in a local department store waiting on customers who were shopping for men's underwear and socks. My job was to assist them in finding what they needed and then to collect their money and wrap the merchandise for them. I worked only on Saturdays, and I lasted about two months.

I did my best, but my heart was never in it. I was in

the wrong place, and I did not like what I was doing. Selling things has never been exciting to me. Although I was not lazy, I longed for the day to end. Even though I was very polite to each customer, my sincerity was forced. I was not committed, and it was a relief when they fired me. I went around the corner to a large grocery store and went to work as a bag boy. I sacked groceries and carried them out to customers' cars. I also swept and mopped the store and helped to display fruits and vegetables. It was hot and sweaty and physically exhausting, and they paid me less than I'd earned at my salesperson's job. But I loved it, and I worked there until I graduated from high school.

SOUL-HUNGER FULFILLS THE WHOLE PERSON Sue Bender reminds us in *Plain and Simple* that when we give ourselves to the process of growth and self-fulfillment, we are not required to surrender a part of ourselves along the way: "I [don't] have to choose one part of me over another," she writes. That is, if an option requires me to deny the existence of a part of myself that I know to be real, I am chasing illusions when I follow that option. If, as an example, being successful requires me to suppress my musical and artistic side, my success will always be an illusion. Or, if I must deny the reality of my sexuality, or my weakness, or any of the feelings I legitimately feel, or if I lose my integrity as a person in order to succeed, I am chasing an illusion.

But, on the other hand, when I follow the hunger of my soul for life, I grow as a total person. For example, Michael Preston was a big-city lawyer who made a lot of money making a lot of money for other people. He finished law school at age thirty and set out to find prosperity and fame. After thirteen years of doing what lawyers do, he realized that there was a big part of him that was not being expressed in his legal work. There was a big hole in the middle of his life. It was less that he objected to what he was doing than that he objected to what he was *not* able to do. He was like a child's puzzle with a missing piece. So he closed up shop and went back to school to earn a master's degree. When he finished his schooling, he went to work as a coach in a school for retarded children. His biggest thrill? He told me that he loves it all but especially loading his kids up in a school bus and taking them to a Special Olympics event. Has he found what was missing, and is he expressing his total being? "I don't think anything's left out," he told me one day when we were discussing it.

SOUL-HUNGER IS FIRSTHAND Soul-hunger can never be a spectator sport. It can never be vicarious. We can no more satisfy our hunger for life by someone else's efforts than we can satisfy physical hunger with food that someone else eats. We must enter the fray for ourselves and experience firsthand what the risks are. To paraphrase a popular TV slogan, we experience firsthand the "thrill of victory and the agony of defeat." No one else can do it for us.

Anthony de Mello, in *The Song of the Bird,* tells of the disciple who complained to his master, "You tell us stories, but you never reveal their meaning to us." The master replied, "How would you like it if someone offered you fruit and chewed it up before giving it to you?" The point of the story, de Mello explains, is that no one can find *our* meaning. He then reminds us that no one ever got drunk on the word "wine."

Soul-hunger is also firsthand in the sense that we can never follow someone else's dream. To be caught up in the fulfillment of another's purposes is death to the soul. We must each acknowledge and follow the deep hunger within our own being. A client told me recently that she had wanted to be an elementary school teacher all her life. Instead, she had grown up to be a highly paid executive in a communications company. She traveled the nation instructing her company's personnel in the intricate computer systems they used. Yet she never lost her desire to teach children to read and write. When I encouraged her to go for her dream, she responded, "I couldn't do that because people expect me to be *somebody*."

She resisted my efforts to help her identify these persons. "I have an image to live up to," she said. She refused to leave my office that day until she had replaced the makeup her tears had washed away. She drove out of the parking lot in her blue BMW and never came back.

SOUL-HUNGER ACKNOWLEDGES OUR LIMITS Soul-hunger never pushes us beyond our personal limits. We are never asked to do anything that is not within the capacity of our own authenticity. Soul-hunger is open and honest, never devious or manipulative. Its intent is never merely to manage impressions. And, when we are guided by this inner integrity, we are never left to explain or justify what we are about.

Winnie-the-Pooh's friend Tigger is an example of someone who is always exceeding personal limits and trying, at great personal cost, to manage impressions. For example, he and Roo were walking through the forest one morning, and Tigger was explaining how Tiggers do virtually everything—and they do it well. Roo, being small and young and not too wise in the ways of the world, was duly impressed. There are, it seems, very few things that Tiggers cannot do, and one thing they do exceptionally well is respond when others are impressed.

"Can they fly?" asked Roo. Tigger could not wait to respond. He explained that they were excellent at flying, and when Roo wanted to know if they could fly as well as birds, Tigger enthusiastically replied that they could, "only they don't want to."

That last statement is a dead giveaway. But Roo didn't spot it, and Tigger continued to explain how talented Tiggers are: " 'Can Tiggers swim?' 'Of course they can. Tiggers can do everything.' 'Can they climb trees better than Pooh?' asked Roo, stopping beneath the tallest Pine Tree, and looking up at it. 'Climbing trees is what they do best,' said Tigger. 'Much better than Poohs.' "

Soon they were up in the tree and couldn't get down. Tiggers may go up trees better than Poohs, but they can't go down, it seems. Tigger was forced to cry out for help. Along came Pooh and Eeyore and Piglet and Christopher Robin who, hearing Tigger's cry of distress, formed a "rescue net." Roo jumped and was safely caught in the net. Tigger fell headlong: "There was a loud crash, and a tearing noise, and a confused heap of everybody on the ground. Christopher Robin and Pooh and Piglet picked themselves up first, and then they picked Tigger up, and underneath everybody else was Eeyore." It was all so embarrassing and there is doubt that Tigger learned any lessons at all.

SOUL-HUNGER SATISFIES When we have found the groove for which our lives have been created, there is an inner quietness and a profound sense of peace within. What we do fits us, and we are comfortable. We have a sense that what we are doing is *worth* doing. We have a sense of gratitude for life; some even feel lucky to be doing what they are doing.

The truth is that in almost any situation, there are any number of possible options that would satisfy and fulfill. Choosing is a matter of being receptive to a direction that involves the freedom of creative choice. No one may live a satisfied life if he or she is not personally and fully free to choose. If our choices are dictated by anyone, they are not choices at all. If we make decisions on that basis we can never be fully satisfied no matter how successful and prosperous we become.

For me, all this means that there is a powerful and revolutionary truth available to each of us. But that truth remains a big secret for a lot of people. Here it is: as we quiet our minds and let go of our fears, as we rid ourselves of the irrational defenses that block us from ourselves, we get in touch with the universal energy that is within us. The little flame of life that flickers in me is the same force that is creating the universe. I am the creative and ingenious expression of life's love of life. I do not have to coerce life to express itself through me. I do not have to control or compel life to love me. All that is required of me is that I not get in the way. And as I fulfill my deepest potential and become all that I can be, the universe is born in me. That is perhaps what Meister Eckhart meant when he said, "We are meant to be the Mother of God."

I witnessed this mystery the morning I watched June Bug's baby take his first step. He found his mother's udder and drank to his heart's content. Everything he needed to take in that warm milk and grow up to become a beautiful and wonderful horse was already there inside him on that first day. It is not hard for me to see that God was being born in that little baby's search for his own life. The universe was coming into being in him.

Becoming everything we are destined to be is a natural process, but that does not mean it is always smooth. There are inevitable bumps and turning points in all our lives. We move from one change to another and from one stage of life to another. Sometimes the changes are sudden and devastating, and at others they are subtle and indirect. Whatever form they take, we can't avoid them. We can't resist them, we can't go around them, and we can't make them go away. We cannot even skip ahead of them.

But I think we can grow through change and experience it with less distress if we allow ourselves to remain receptive to the natural hunger of our soul for life. As D. H. Lawrence wrote, in "Why the Novel Matters" "out of the full play of all things emerges the only thing that is anything"— a whole person.

Chapter 8

❖

PEOPLE OF THE HEART

"I don't know enough," replied the Scarecrow
cheerfully. "My head is stuffed with straw, you know,
and that is why I am going to Oz to ask him for some
brains."

"Oh, I see," said the Tin Woodman. "But after all,
brains are not the best thing in the world."

"Have you any?" inquired the Scarecrow.

"No, my head is quite empty," answered the Tin
Woodman. "But I once had brains, and a heart also;
so having tried them both, I should much rather have
a heart."

—*THE WIZARD OF OZ*

❖ *Some people have trouble*
with their hearts. For them, only knowledge that comes
through the senses is valid, because they have no inner eye.
They are unaware of the mind of the heart. People like that
are usually the ones who have trouble with joy. That is
because our hearts are the avenue of the soul and the path
by which joy comes into our lives.

Jamake Highwater, in his wonderful book on the mind of Native Americans entitled *The Primal Mind,* relates the advice of an elderly Native American he interviewed one day. Worried that Highwater was too preoccupied with the rational mind and with words, the old man earnestly admonished:

> You must learn to look at the world twice. . . . First you must bring your eyes together in front so you can see each droplet of rain on the grass, so you can see the smoke rising from an anthill in the sunshine. *Nothing* should escape your notice. But you must learn to look again, with your eyes at the very edge of what is visible. Now you must see dimly if you wish to see things that are dim—visions, mist, and cloud-people . . . animals which hurry past you in the dark. You must learn to look at the world twice if you wish to see all that there is to see.

Highwater called this second look at the edge of visibility the "ability to see a second world." Seeing dimly in order to see things that are not on the surface is what the heart does. As reported in John Neihardt's *Black Elk Speaks,* Black Elk, a Sioux medicine man, was seeing with the heart when he reported, "While I stood there I saw more than I can tell and I understood more than I saw: for I was seeing in a sacred manner the shapes of all things in the spirit, and the shape of all shapes as they must live together like one being."

The world of the heart sees more than it can explain, more even than it can understand. It sees and communes with the simple and the quiet, the natural, the plain, and the commonplace. The heart can act spontaneously and without premeditation. The heart really *sees.* It really *hears.* When we look with the eyes of the heart and hear with its ears, we find the beauty that surrounds us in everything. We welcome questions as much as answers. We are present in our own lives.

Centuries ago Augustine warned about looking only with the eyes. He said, "People travel to wonder at the height of mountains, at the huge waves of the sea, at the long courses of rivers, at the vast compass of the ocean, at the circular motion of the stars; and they pass by themselves without wondering." His wise words remind us that we can be so involved in faraway things and future possibilities that we miss the wonder of the things in the here and now, including ourselves.

Bernard Shaw doubtless had these ideas in mind as one of his characters said, "When I went to those great cities I saw wonders I had never seen in Ireland. But when I came back to Ireland I found all the wonders there waiting for me. You see they had been there all the time; but my eyes had never been opened to them. I did not know what my own house looked like, because I had never been outside it."

Harvard psychologist Michael Maccoby found heart trouble to be characteristic of our society. In his book, *The Gamesman,* he reported on a seven-year study of 250 high-tech managers and executives and found that these people, both men and women, had highly developed cognitive and intellectual skills. They were accomplished and competent in a business sense. But, in Maccoby's words, they were spiritually and emotionally stunted. They could neither give nor receive love, and most of them lacked the courage to be real. Maccoby determined that these persons had "highly developed heads and underdeveloped hearts." He concluded with an appeal to American business leaders to develop their hearts along with their heads.

People who lack heart are frequently people who still need the hurts of earlier heartbreak to be healed. Their soul has been diminished by the pain and hurt of previous losses. To use a biblical phrase, "Their heart has been hardened." They are truly emotionally and spiritually stunted. Here are some of the problems they confront in life:

They cannot risk.
They are poor at relationships.
They have trouble with love.
They find it hard to trust.
They have trouble knowing what normal is.
They are ruled by fear.
They sincerely believe that they do not deserve good things.
They are paranoid.
They are troubled sexually.
Regardless of how much they accomplish, they never feel like a success.
They have no sense of fun or adventure in their life.
They experience little joy.

How do we open ourselves up to that self-fulfilling inclination that exists within the soul, and how do we learn to look at the world twice? How do we unlearn our culture's emphasis on the eye of the mind and open ourselves up to the eyes of the heart? How do we overcome our learned fear of the intuitive mind and rediscover our soul's capacity for the spirit-world and all those wonderful things that exist at the edge of visibility? How do we overcome the habit of existence and develop a lust for life?

A friend of mine, Betty Louise Martin Davis had these questions in mind when she asked:

O tiny heart within my soul
Can you beat enough to make a flow of tears
To wash away the sands of time
And heal the hurts within my mind?

Join the Dance of Creation

In the Hindu religion, the great God Shiva "dances" creation. It is playful work, not onerous labor. And it is an ongoing act, not something that is ever really over. Its purpose is the sheer joy of the dance itself. God is the eternal dancer; creation is his dance, and he proceeds to dance because that is what he does. He is continually dancing, and he offers us the opportunity to join the dance with him.

The opening chapters of the Old Testament paint a similar portrait of the same spontaneous, joyful, and cavorting creator. The spirit of God broods over the waters like a mother's warm embrace gently caressing the universe into being. The spirit punctuates the creative process with frequent and delighted announcements that all is good. Light is separated from dark, moisture kisses the soil, and life comes. Plants, then animals, and finally the frolicking spirit calls humankind into being. A garden of peaceful delight is home, and all created things exist in joyful union with themselves, with one another, and with the creator.

TOUCHING THE TREES Suzanne Hales is familiar with this connection with creation. She recently attended a week-long seminar in a rural area of New York state. For some reason unknown to her she did not feel a part of the small group that attended the seminar. It was not a good experience for her, and she felt lonely and left out. She sensed that the other persons in the group were judging her and that she was not playing the game to their satisfaction.

After about three days of experiencing these feelings, she left the group for a short walk in the woods that surrounded the encampment where the seminar was being held. It was Mother's Day, and being alone in the woods among the massive trees seemed only to increase her sense of isolation and loneliness.

She wanted to be home, and in her restlessness and soul-searching she felt drawn to an enormous birch tree. She looked intently at its rough, grayish bark, observing the deep grooves that wove their way through the rich texture of the trunk. She saw the mighty, outswept limbs above her and the intense green of the shimmering leaves. High, white clouds rushed from her left to her right, and looking up into that sky was, for her, like staring into a bottomless blue pit. She smelled the rich, moist, pungent odor of the forest around her.

She reached out with her arms to hug the tree. She felt the tree's strength, its quiet power, and the rough bark against her face and body. She felt herself flow into the center of the tree and become one with the life-force of the tree. She felt herself swept downward into the roots of the tree and knew each tiny opening through which the tree received the earth's sweet nourishment. As part of the life of the tree, she floated upward into the limbs and became each rippling leaf. She felt the wind and drank the gentle warmth of the sunlight.

Finally, she returned to herself, embracing the tree from the outside. She hugged, but she felt hugged. The tree took her in and embraced her. She knew she was where she belonged, and in that moment she knew that she was home.

In *The Unheard Cry for Meaning,* Viktor Frankl tells of another young woman who, in extremely adverse circumstances, knew the joy of this dance. Critically ill and imprisoned in Auschwitz, she knew, as did he, that she would die in a few days. Pointing out the window of the hut, she said, "This tree is the only friend I have in my loneliness." Her reference was to a single branch of the chestnut tree that she could see through the window. "I often talk to this tree," she commented. Frankl reports that he was startled by her words and didn't know how to respond. He wondered, Was she delirious? Was she hallucinating? Not knowing what else to say, he asked her if the tree answered her when she talked to it. She nodded affirmatively, and when Frankl asked her what it said, she answered, "It says to me, 'I am here—I am here—I am life, eternal life.' "

What is a walk in the country for us? Or, for that matter, what is a walk through the city, or in our backyard, or in our own home? Do we find anything in that landscape that is, for us, marvelously rich and significant? Do we know, in any personal way, what it is like to be a daisy or a breaking wave or even the mysterious moon itself? Can we get inside the skin of an animal or an insect or a plant and tell with any convincing detail how it feels and how its experience of life is like, or unlike, our own?

SEEING, NOT JUST LOOKING   But, we respond, we have looked at thousands of trees and heard thousands of birds and seen thousands of bugs. Have we? Or have we only registered in our minds the labels of *tree* and *bird* and *bug*? To see, we must *see*. How much of our seeing is blind because our experience is indirect? We take whatever is in front of us and place it into a category that seems appropriate to us. In so doing, we miss the reality of the thing itself because our only experience is of the thing as category.

We can relate to everything in our lives in this manner, including people. Instead of experiencing the individual we encounter, we see only a category. For example, if I meet a woman who is an executive at a life insurance company, I can label her in any of the following ways. She is a woman, she is an executive, and she works in the insurance field. I can place her into an age category and a race category. I can classify her education, income, and geographical region. I can assume things about her religion, her femininity, and her interests. I can even assume that I know how she will respond to me as a person. At each step of this process, she is forced into my preset designations. I may talk to her for hours, weeks, or months without ever knowing her. What I will experience is the confirmation of whatever labels I hang on her. But I do not experience the person she is. And I lose twice when I experience this person indirectly: first, I miss knowing her as a person; and second, this process shuts me down and blocks my opportunity to try new things and grow as a person.

Frederick Franck, in *The Zen of Seeing,* quotes a woman who has learned that there is a difference between looking at things and seeing them. She says, "I am a widow and live alone, and I often feel lonely. Today I learned that if you really see the things around you, you're not lonely anymore." How much of our loneliness and isolation comes as a result of our inability to see because we only experience things as categories?

SEEING WITH THE HEART Jamake Highwater relates the story of a Zuni Indian who saw clearly the dangers of attaching preconceived labels to things around us. She asked an ethnologist who was meticulously recording each word of a traditional story, "When I tell these stories, do you *see* it, or do you just write it down?"

When we are little, we see with the heart and dance easily and naturally. But when we grow up we find it hard to do. We become thinkers and planners and judges. We get tunnel vision and become goal-oriented. We bend our wonderful rationality toward the narrow end of achieving material goals. We talk too much, and we dance too little. We forget the wisdom from *The Little Prince* that "it is only with the heart that one can see clearly."

This dance cannot be bottled and saved for later. If we fail to dance the dance, for us it does not exist. There are no doggy bags that we can put it into and take home to enjoy later. Like the manna that the children of Israel received while in the wilderness, we must gather our allotment each day, for that day and no more. We cannot collect enough today to last a week, or a lifetime. Dancing creation is done one day at a time.

We fall short when we fail to see with the heart and join the creation dance. No matter what else is true for our lives, our souls shrivel up and we miss our joy. Let us be silent and contemplate the dance of creation around us. We can look at a star, a flower, a fading leaf, a bird, a stone, a child, our hands, our feet, our legs, another person. These are fragments of the dance, and we can join in.

Richard Erdoes, in *Lame Deer—Seeker of Visions,* reports that Lame Deer, a Sioux medicine man, encourages us to enter the dance with these words: "Let's sit down here, all of us, on the open prairie . . . no blankets to sit on, but feel the ground with our bodies, the earth, the yielding shrubs. Let's have the grass for a mattress, experiencing its sharpness and its softness. Let us become like stones, plants, and trees. Let us be animals, think and feel like animals."

Embrace the Sweetness in Everything

In *Letters to a Young Poet,* Rainer Maria Rilke offered gentle solace to a lonely and unsettled friend who had lost contact with his soul because he had lost a sense of God's presence in his life. Among the many words of wisdom that Rilke offered are these: "By extracting the most possible sweetness out of everything, just as the bees gather honey, we thus build Him."

When we choose to extract the sweetness out of every situation, we provide a channel through which the inner spirit can be more fully realized. We discover our life in everything. The operative phrase here is "in every situation." We are really alive when we can accomplish the difficult task of apprehending our life in all that is around us and perceive life and fullness and joy in all our affairs and in all that happens in our life. The truth is that we fail to be aware of most that is going on around us, and we evaluate and judge what we do allow in our conscious mind.

FINDING LIFE IN EVERY LITTLE THING   To be alive is not to withdraw from or filter out any aspects of life. The Zen Master, when he attained enlightenment, said, "Oh wondrous marvel: I chop wood! I draw water from the well!" People who are joyfully alive are into chopping wood and drawing water if in fact chopping wood and drawing water are in their lives. When we are alive, we do not attempt to dodge or escape any part of our lives. Rather, we *wonder* in each of these experiences. They delight and intrigue us, and they bring joy to us for no other reason than that they are in our lives. We are *into* them, and they both fill up and express our souls. That is surely the meaning of the old Rabbinical story in which a disciple asks the rabbi, "In the olden days, people saw the face of God. Why don't we do that today?" The old rabbi responds, "Because no one is willing to stoop that low."

Martin Buber said, "All suffering prepares the soul for vision." This great man of uncommon wisdom was, as usual, correct in this evaluation of the place of suffering in human growth. Our struggles open us up to fullness and transformation, if we are willing to allow this evolution to occur. But what Buber so insightfully observed about suffering could be said of every experience of life. Nothing occurs that is without meaning and that cannot prepare our souls for vision.

In *Letters to a Young Poet,* Rilke counsels us to have the courage to look into everything to find our higher self. He admonishes us to experience our existence "as broadly as we can," finding ourselves in everything, "even the unheard-of," the "most inexplicable," and "the most strange." This, he asserts, is the only courage that is demanded of us. But, Rilke continues, instead of being courageous, humankind has been cowardly, and our cowardice "has done life endless harm." We have lost our ability to have "visions" and have lost contact with "the whole so-called spirit-world, death, all those things that are so closely akin to us." The result, he continues, is that these most significant and meaningful human experiences "have by daily parrying been so crowded out of life that the senses with which we would have grasped them are atrophied."

SAVING THE BITTER AND THROWING OUT THE SWEET Rilke, it seems to me, is saying that we have lost the ability to recognize and feed the hunger of the soul. Our inner passageways, through which life's most meaningful experiences must travel to become reality for us, have significantly deteriorated. The sad fact is that most of us attempt to extract the sweetness *out*. That is, we keep the bitter and throw the sweetness away. For example, I met with a small circle of friends recently to close out a series of discussion meetings we had been having. We had agreed to meet for four months to share and support each other's transformation. We planned to take a few weeks off before continuing the meetings. One of our members, a young mother of three small children, was not remaining in the group. She and her family were moving out of the state. Her husband had been transferred, and for the first time she was going to live somewhere other than the city where she had been born and had grown up. She was excited and happy about the move and the prospects for her life, but at the same time she was apprehensive and worried. She was also sorrowful about leaving our group, and we were sad to see her go.

In the process of closing out the group, several people told her how much she meant to them. They spoke of "caring" for her, "admiring" her, and being "excited" about her growth and self-discovery. They were all sincere, and some were even tearful. They spoke of "loving" her. It was an emotional moment for me. I felt very close to this young woman, and although I did not say a word, I could have expressed everything that the others said.

Her response, however, was surprising to me. She seemed embarrassed and appeared to want it all to end. She reacted with self-deprecating statements and humor in which she put herself down. She squirmed and twisted nervously in her seat. She effectively cut off every person who addressed her. She seemed to want to redirect the process whenever she was the object of affectionate attention. She was being loved by a very caring "family," and she was not taking it in. She sabotaged the process.

How do we stop ourselves from extracting sweetness?

- We expect the worst. When we notice a problem, we begin a "worst case scenario" with a list of "what ifs." This is called *catastrophizing*.
- We personalize everything. We come to believe that everything people do or say is directed at us. We think they are trying to give us "messages" through their actions.
- We "should" ourselves and others. Our shoulds exist as a long list of unwritten but ironclad rules about how we and other people should act. We resent others who break our rules and we feel guilty, or spend enormous rationalizing energy, when we fail to live up to our shoulds.
- We get into the other people's minds and know, without asking, what they are thinking. We use mind reading to determine what other people are feeling toward us, and we respond on the basis of our expectations. We assume we know why they act the way they do. And when the inevitable confusion arises out of this muddle, our predictions are confirmed as self-fulfilling prophecy, and we say, "I knew it all the time."
- We take in criticism and block out compliments. We even magnify the negative and minimize the positive. We believe that people are sincere (and correct) when they criticize and insincere when they compliment us.
- We see everything in black and white. Only two extremes exist for us. One is good and the other is bad, and nothing exists between the two. Either we are perfect, or we are a failure. There is no middle ground.

- We compare. We are constantly analyzing other people and comparing ourselves to them. We try to determine who's smarter, more competent, younger-looking, more prepared, better educated, and so on.
- We overgeneralize. We reach general conclusions based on a single incident or piece of evidence. For example, if someone disappoints us, we expect that person always to disappoint us. Soon we expect everyone to disappoint us. Or, once something bad happens, we expect it to happen over and over again.
- We blame. We need someone other than ourselves to hold responsible for our pain. Or, conversely, we blame ourselves for everything. One woman friend of mine said, only half-kidding, "I am responsible for the rust on the Statue of Liberty."
- We insist that nothing change. We seek stability and want permanence. The threat of change in ourselves or others is terrifying. We believe that if we are diligent enough, we can make everything remain the same. Then, and only then, we will be safe.
- We must always be right and never be wrong. We live life as if it were a courtroom trial, trying constantly to prove that our ideas, opinions, actions, and attitudes are correct. Being wrong is unthinkable, and we go to any length to demonstrate that we are right.

The challenge is to reverse these processes and reawaken the inner pathways necessary to discover the more meaningful parts of our life. We can quiet our appetites for the tinsel and light that we have internalized from our culture and religion and civilization. We can rediscover the joy and excitement of life and the honeylike sweetness that is in every situation in our lives. We can satisfy the soul-hunger within.

Try a small experiment in your life and see if it does

not begin to open you up to the sweetness that is every-where around you. Sit, close your eyes, and lay your arms, palms up, easily on your legs. Slowly raise your hands, still with palms up, until they are about shoulder height. Gently extend your arms to full length. After a few moments, and when you are ready, slowly lower your hands until they are again resting on your legs. What did this exercise feel like to you? Was there a feeling of receiving? What did you receive? What can you take away from this exercise?

Live the Questions, Not the Answers

Most of the time we think that living with questions instead of answers is a miserable experience. We like everything regulated, nailed down, figured out. We do not like things open-ended, inconclusive, or unresolved. Questions leave us unsettled.

What we want is control; and needing to have all the answers is, in essence, an aspect of that desire. We cut life into patterns, small and simple sections, in order to control it. Any unresolved part leaves us feeling unsure, as if we were not in command. We need to know precisely what the destination is and what is going to happen to us.

Of course, any sense of control we may have is, at best, an illusion. The reality is that there are more questions than answers. What will happen to us along the way, even at the next step, is always an unknown. To live with joy is to learn that we can live the questions and that they are, in the final analysis, more important than the answers.

Sue Monk Kidd, in her book *When the Heart Waits*, asks us to stop suppressing our questions and embrace them. She borrows Rilke's phrase and asks us to "live our questions." She states, "There's an art to living your questions. You peel them. You listen to them. You let them spawn new questions. You hold the unknowing inside. You linger with it instead of rushing into half-baked answers."

It is in living the questions that we discover our lost hunger for life because questions raise us above mere existence. The people who help make our lives exciting are the ones who push us into consideration and contemplation by asking questions rather than answering them. They punctuate our lives with question marks rather than periods and lead us to exclamation marks.

Friedrich Nietzsche, the nineteenth-century philosopher, once commented, "Madness does not come from uncertainty, rather it comes from certainty." He knew that questions are a good thing and that having all the answers makes life boring and unfulfilling. Maybe that is what Jesus meant when he said, "Ask and you shall receive." Most of us interpret that remark as "Ask for whatever you want and you will get it." Maybe he meant that we should live our questions more. Perhaps it is the simple act of waiting in the darkness of an unanswered question that opens us to the answer.

Anthony de Mello, in *The Heart of the Enlightened*, writes, "Some people will never learn anything because they grasp too soon. Wisdom, after all, is not a station you arrive at but a manner of traveling. . . . To know exactly where you are headed may be the best way to go astray. Not all who loiter are lost." No one is so ignorant as the person who knows all the answers, and no one so lost as the person who thinks he knows exactly where he is.

In her poem "Do Not Ask Me" Karen Frances encourages us to become more aware of questions, especially those that love asks:

Do not ask me... For I do not know.
Wisdom comes with age, they say,
so I suppose I should know.

But I tell you, I have no answer.
What is the meaning of life,
this never ending struggle?
God in the Heavens?
I tell you I do not know.
Should I, shouldn't I?
Will I, won't I?
Yes or no, when or how, do not ask me...

But there is one thing I have.
It's not an answer. It's a question.
And that is love.

How well are we living our questions? Please consider the following, and when you are ready briefly write out your responses:

1. What is the question to which your life is the answer?

2. What are the important questions that love asks? (Consider, as examples, the following: How can I love me? How can I love you? How can I love life? How can I love God? How can I love the earth? What is worthy of my love? How can I not waste my love? How can my love matter?)

3. What are the really important questions in life? What are the questions that you *must* answer?

(Some of the important questions you might ask are these: What would it mean for me really to love? How am I experiencing life right now? What darkness in me needs to be illuminated and transformed? Where do I need more honesty? What am I doing with my sexuality? What is the meaning of my life? What am I living for?)

4. What are your unanswered questions?

5. How are you doing at "living your questions"?

Be Present in Your Life

A participant at a workshop on the art of living life to the fullest had just been asked to draw a picture of something she loved. She chose to draw a geranium, her favorite flower. When she finished, she told the group, "I have grown geraniums for thirty years, but, believe it or not, I never knew what a geranium looked like."

This person illustrates the modern dilemma that may

be described as not being present in our own lives. We are so focused on what is to come or on what has already been that we miss what is directly in front of us. We look but do not see; we listen but do not hear; we eat but do not taste; we touch but do not connect. Living this way, we miss our own being.

We believe that we must hurry in order to live every minute to the fullest. So we rush around to catch all the action we can. Maybe we need to switch off the world and come back to earth for a spell. Of course, we're all busy. We have to be to make a living, meet our obligations, and keep from being run over or left behind. But, we can learn to stop our hurry and cease rushing around. We can sit quietly on the grass to allow ourselves to notice a tree, a bird, a cloud, a leaf. When we do, we create time for our soul to catch up.

FEAR AND LOSS AS PREDICTION Sometimes we believe that the fears of the past can successfully prophesy those of the future. The results of this type of thinking are that we spend most of our time worrying about the past or the future. We live in a vicious circle of fear that leaves little room for love and joy in the present. This type of thinking can overwhelm us. At times, we feel comfortable predicting that we are going to be miserable the next moment, and then find pleasure in being right. It is as if we would rather have the pleasure of being right than have true happiness in the present moment.

Angelicas of Silesius, a seventeenth-century mystic, warned us about the temptation to live our lives in the future:

> In good time we shall see
> God and his light, you say.
> Fool, you shall never see
> What you do not see today!

Centuries earlier, a biblical writer advised, "Be still and know that I am God." Here is Buddha's secret on how to do that: He traveled all of India to find enlightenment and tried everything under the sun, to no avail. Then one day he sat under the Bodhi tree, and enlightenment came to him. When asked what the secret was, he responded: "When you draw in a deep breath, oh monks, be aware that you are drawing in a deep breath. And when you draw in a shallow breath, oh monks, be aware that you are drawing in a shallow breath. And when you draw in a medium-sized breath, oh monks, be aware that you are drawing in a medium-sized breath."

SLOW DOWN AND LET LIFE CATCH UP Buddhism teaches the principle of awareness. Whatever I am doing, I am aware of all the sensations of the *present*. Let us say that I am washing dishes. Instead of seeing this task as unpleasant and hurrying through it in order to get on with something fun, I experience the sensations of each act of washing. I feel the warm water on my hands, I see the gleam of the dish, I feel the dish in my hand. I force myself to be aware of each aspect of the process of washing dishes. In such a way, I am absorbed in the present.

Absorption in the present is the key to being still. Nothing beats slowing down and living in the *now*. We need less to enrich our lives than to slow down long enough to discover the treasure that is already there. Thus the question becomes, How present are we in our lives? Let's consider the following questions:

1. List three things you can do to slow down your life.

2. There is an old saying that advises, "Take time to smell the roses along the way." Name some of the roses that you are hurrying past.

3. It is good once in a while to turn off pressure and demands that you impose on yourself. What are three kinds of pressure that you can take off yourself?

4. It is healthy to be aware and tolerant of your own limitations and mistakes. What are three limitations of yours of which you can be more accepting and aware? Will this help you reduce self-criticism?

5. Finally, it is always good to love yourself and be kind and gentle with yourself. What are three little kindnesses you may do to love and nurture yourself?

My friend Chris Watts is a commercial real estate sales-man. He's thirty, divorced, and searching for his soul. He's been trying to slow down and live in the present and to see with more than his eyes. He went fishing the other day and had quite an experience. Here, in his own words, is what happened to him:

It was dawn when I arrived at a small pond where I had fished many times before. A slight fog rose from the water's surface and shrouded the trees in a quiet blanket. The sun, pushing through an overlay of clouds in the eastern sky, threw glimmerings of light across the water's surface. The air was filled with si-lence and everything was still. My heart warmed with a sense of inner peace as I drank in the hushed grace and beauty of the place.

Fishing, I decided, would disturb the setting. So I sat on the grass by the pond's edge, my back against a large willow. Closing my eyes, I concentrated on my breathing. It felt good to relax and leave behind the stress and worry of a cluttered mind that I had lived with for the past few weeks. I felt my facial muscles relax and then the tightness of my shoulders and arms slowly drain out through my fingers. I loosened and calmed the muscles of my legs and feet and then re-turned to my breathing.

I had no conscious thought of which I was aware. It was like my mind was empty, all thought and power of reason poured out like water from a glass. Suddenly, I noticed all the different sounds around me. Before, when I first arrived at the pond, I had heard only the silence. Now, all the sounds of life about me pushed themselves into my emptied mind. I heard the birds, crickets, frogs, wind, leaves. I heard the splashing of the fish and I even heard the limbs swaying above me. I heard everything. As I continued to listen, I felt myself melt into life. I became the things I was hearing. They were inside me and outside me at one and the same time. I lost sensation of my physical body, myself as a separate identity. I was listening and at the same time I was that which I was hearing. I was lost in the experience of being alive.

As I opened my eyes, I felt the sensation of returning. I had to readjust to the sense of being a physical body. I had to refocus my eyes to see the things about me. I saw a fish swimming in the water and I knew that it was doing exactly what a fish was supposed to do. It was being a fish. I heard a bird in the distance and knew that the bird was free to be a bird. I felt the willow's rough bark on my back and knew that the tree was being what God intended it to be. The sun, the clouds, and each living thing around me was living in harmony with that inner pattern. I felt a freedom and a unity with life. I wondered about my life. How much of what I do is just doing what Chris is doing and how much is fighting the natural mechanisms of living? In that moment, I was aware of the process of life and myself as a part of that process. I realized that I had never before been so alive as when I was lost in the union with all of life in that experience.

Chris was overwhelmed with this experience. For the first time in his adult life, he saw with his heart. "I want more," he told me later. "Can I live like this?" he asked.

❖

ℒIVING THE JOY
OF THE SOUL

Those who are mentally and emotionally healthy are
those who have learned when to say yes, when to say
no, and when to say whoopee.

—WILLARD S. KRABILL

❖ *We don't even know her*
name. The Hebrew scriptures call her only a "Levite
woman." But she is a courageous person whom we may all
admire and emulate.

She gave birth to a beautiful boy-child, her firstborn
son, in the land of Egypt shortly after the Pharaoh had
ordered all male Hebrew babies to be killed at birth. This
cruel decree from the all-powerful despot struck fear in the
hearts of all pregnant Hebrew women and the midwives
who assisted them at birth. And according to the record in
the Old Testament, most obeyed to save their own lives. But
not this unnamed woman.

She took her life in her own hands and, filled with the
determination that love alone can produce, wove a small
basket of bulrushes, made it watertight with clay and tar,
and hid her baby in the reeds at the water's edge of the Nile.
What exactly she hoped to accomplish and how she
planned to raise this child in the plain sight of both Hebrew

and Egyptian neighbors, she did not know. She knew only that she would not let them kill her baby. She stationed her daughter nearby to ensure that no hurt befell him.

Only a few days passed before the Pharaoh's daughter, coming to bathe, discovered the child. Perhaps this discovery by the Egyptian princess was a part of the young mother's plan. We do not know. What we do know is that, moved perhaps as much by the mother's courage as the child's beauty, the Pharaoh's daughter took him in and raised him as her own son. She called the mother to nurse the child, and she gave him a Hebrew name, *Moshen*. We know him by the name of Moses.

This Levite woman had what D. H. Lawrence called in "Why the Novel Matters," an "instinct for life." She knew that although we choose few, if any, of the circumstances of our life, we can choose our reactions to them. Life isn't automatic and does not stand still for any of us. Rather, life commands that we be alive. It moves like a fast-flowing river that demands that we move also. Not to move is to be inert, and inertia kills. Equally fatal is the temptation to try to stop the river. We grow and change, things come and go, we take chances, some of which we win and some we lose. We grieve and move on, or we die. This brave Levite woman, by her choice, ensured the life of her own son and perhaps all of Judeo-Christian history. Her instinct for life provided her with an appetite to engage life. She saw her problems as challenges, she knew that all that life requires of us is our best, and she spurned a problem-free life as no life at all. She refused to play it safe. She took action in a spirit of quiet determination. She knew that what counts is being ourselves in the rowdy motion of life. That is what the joy of the soul is all about.

So she jumped into the commotion. Her inspiring act encourages us in three important ways:

1. We must at times take the most difficult path. The Levite woman was not afraid to take the hard road,

even in the face of almost certain odds that she could do nothing but fail.

2. We must find the courage to be ourselves. The woman had the fortitude to be herself and refused to conform to the will of the majority. Rather, she left the pack and pursued her own goals.

3. Sometimes we must go against popular expectations. The young mother defied powerful social norms and rules of behavior. In a sense, she suspended what she considered to be inhumane rules and wrote her own, then she lived her life according to those.

Let's take a look at each of these ways of surviving and see how we may apply her example to our own lives.

Take the Hard Way

Almost all the great religions of the world have, in one way or another, described the path to inner growth and the discovery of the self as difficult. That is why, in the words of Robert Frost, it is the road less traveled. Yet, it is the only road that is worth traveling. To take it is to commence the "great turning" that will render our lives different forever. It alone is the path that leads toward the home at the center of our being.

THE HARD WAY OFFERS THE GIFT OF TEARS   The birth of the soul is the way of tears. That statement is true despite our difficulty in grasping the association of new life with sorrow and weeping. Death and life, and therefore new growth and sorrow, are not separate but intertwined. Every stage of a plant's growth from a seed to a tiny plant to a mature stalk is in reality the process of both life and death. The seed dies as it gives up its structure and being to become the tiny plant. The tiny plant dies as it gives up its structure to become the sapling. The sapling dies as it becomes the mature plant producing fruit. The fruit dies as it gives up its structure and being to begin the whole process over again.

Certain death awaits us as we begin to be born, no less so than for the seed thrown into the dark earth. Here are a few of the things that must die in every human being who would grow:

- We are required to give up the defenses that we have developed to protect ourselves and our ego from loss. The rigid structure of our lives, so carefully erected and held in place with desperate tenacity, must collapse.

- The values, prejudices, resentments, and desires that have been at the center of our lives must come crumbling to the ground.

- The masks that we have used to shield our self from both the public and the private view must be discarded because they are no longer adequate to hide behind. We must surrender the old "impressions" that we sought so carefully to present to others and that we ourselves tried to believe.

- Our internal censors, those shields through which reality is filtered so as to screen out painful and unwanted perceptions, must break down. The barrier between the conscious and the unconscious must fall; and the images of the past, with their denied emotions and repressed functions, must flood to the surface.

The loss of these structures does not come without grief, pain, and uncertainty. When we take up this way of going, we are like a person who has walked on crutches for years and now, recognizing that he has never needed them, tosses them aside. Having discarded our crutches, we stand teetering, not really knowing how to walk without them or whether our muscles can hold us up. We have given up the old defenses and illusions that have served to protect our ego but have not yet replaced them with new and healthy structures. In the words of an unknown sage, "First we jump and then we get our wings."

The gift of tears is a genuine *gift*. Weeping has three functions, according to Alan Jones, in *Soul Making*. Tears soften the hard and dried-out soul. They clear the mind. And they open the heart. In his wonderful poem "Things Not Solved though Tomorrow Came" Henry Taylor explains that tears, even those that are not shed, can soften the soul and open the heart. The poem tells about his cross-country trip to deliver his daughter to the boarding school she attends. There is a melancholy that is sensed rather than explicitly described in the poem. Leaving his daughter takes a piece of his own soul from him. It reveals the emptiness, alienation, and sadness of his whole life.

Driving through the lonely night as he returns home, he stops for a bite to eat in a small café. There he meets a young woman, only slightly older than his daughter. She, as it turns out, is a lost and lonely person too. They sit and talk, an island in a sea of loneliness.

> Hours, cigarettes, and cups of coffee
> Find us sitting at this table still,
> Her fingers touching mine.

At closing time they leave together in his car.

> Daughter, love, I see in her
> Eyes a thing I have not seen in yours,
> A thing no one I've loved has let me see
> For years. We do not speak.

They stop at a motel and reach out toward each other in a futile effort to make the love for which they both hunger. They have sex mostly in silence and in the dark. Sleep comes, and when he awakens, he is alone again. Even the masquerade of closeness, which the night gave him, now is gone.

> I rise from bed and take the road once more. The car
> Rolls through the darkness
> > as a fierce beast runs through cold,
> Extinguishing a whispered calling in my ear.
> Of what is past, I only know what I am told—
> I can no longer tell whose voice is in the air.
> Headlights try for secrets the road will always hold:
> There are things I have not seen
> > though I have been to where they are.

The experience of this sad man in Taylor's poem underscores that the masks must be torn away before we can truly see our selves. Birth comes only with the courage to look squarely at what is real in our lives. To avoid the gift of tears is to avoid being born.

The gift of tears is the gift of learning to live without our defenses. They, in truth, are the shams and delusions about which Thoreau warned. Giving them up allows us to discover and live from our deepest needs. We uncover our deep needs and begin the painful search for the courage and integrity that will allow us to get these needs met for the first time in life.

The gift of tears is the valley of the shadow of death, the point at which the seed falls into the darkness of the earth to die. It is the beginning of the discovery of the self, but it *feels* like the loss of the self. It is the beginning of life, but it feels like the end. It is birth, but it feels like death.

THE HARD WAY IS THE GIFT OF LETTING GO In the brief story of Moses' mother, nothing stands out so much as her ability to let go. The truth is that she had to surrender her son at every step of the way.

Joanna Field reminds us, in *A Life of One's Own*, that if we are to have a life that is truly our own, we must learn to "let go." She says that this letting-go is more a feminine than a masculine characteristic. Indeed, she marks her true realization of her own femininity at the point where she discovered the delight that accompanies giving up control and the need to have a specific outcome. She spoke of this even in radical terms, referring to it as a loss of "identity."

In his poem entitled "The Need To Win" Chuang Tzu clearly saw our tendency to manage events and addressed the paradoxical wisdom of surrendering control. When there is nothing to lose and an archer is "shooting for nothing," he has all his skills. But when he shoots for a reward like a "brass buckle," he gets nervous. A prize of gold makes him "blind." He "sees two targets," Chuang Tzu declares, and "is out of his mind." The prize does not lessen his skill. Rather, it "divides him," and he thinks more of winning "than of shooting." The "the need to win drains him of power."

Master Chuang advocates, like Lao Tzu before him, the principle of *Wu Wei,* a term that means literally "without doing, causing, or making." It is often translated by the words *nondoing* or *nonaction*. Practically speaking, what it means is to act without egotistical, meddlesome, or conflictual effort. One acts within the principle of *Wu Wei* when one goes with the flow, not against it. When we are in the nonaction of *Wu Wei*, our actions appear effortless. In his book *The Tao of Pooh*, Benjamin Hoff notes that the Chinese character *Wei* comes from the symbols of the clawing hand of a monkey. That is significant, he says, perhaps with tongue in cheek, because *Wu Wei* means that we stop "monkeying around" and begin to go with the nature of things.

In my own experience, this first stage of joy is the way of many beginnings. It is as if each step strengthens us to continue, and each pathway introduces us to challenging new insights into ourselves. As Edna St. Vincent Millay reminded us, life is the process of being "born anew each day."

THE HARD WAY IS THE GIFT OF DISCOVERY Somewhere in this process, at different times for different people, the light begins to break. Enlightenment takes place. The anxiety and worry that the darkness has brought are turned into awe. We turn to our center and find ourselves, others, and God in that deep, inner space. Life itself becomes different. This is what Dag Hammarskjold meant when in *Markings* he described the changes that this growth made in his life: "I came to a time and place where I realized that the Way leads to a triumph which is a catastrophe and to a catastrophe which is a triumph, that the price for committing one's life would be reproach, and that the only elevation possible to man lies in the depths of humiliation. After that, the word 'courage' lost its meaning, since nothing could be taken from me." New definitions of ourselves and our situations come into play when we enter this stage. Reality does not change. What changes is how we perceive reality and respond to it. Our limitations and weaknesses do not devastate us; and our failures, which continue to occur in our lives, take on much less importance. By the same token our strengths and accomplishments become less significant. I realize that I am neither my failure *nor* my accomplishments. A marvelous freedom emerges from this realization: since I must neither avoid failure nor achieve perfection, I am free to be me! There is peace and rest in losing the self we have had to protect for so many years and finding the authentic self that, while imperfect and weak, no longer needs to be concealed.

Dorothy Dickson Reshel was eleven years old when she described this freedom in the following poem. Today she is an ordained United Methodist minister and has a Ph.D. in clinical psychology.

ME—A QUESTION

Am I afraid to be me?
Why?
Why am I afraid to be
the only thing I can be?
Am I afraid
that if I am me,
if I find out who me is
I will be disappointed?
Am I afraid that the
person I think is me is
someone else?
Why?
Why don't I know who the
real me is?
Why?
Why have I tried
to fool so many people that
I have fooled myself?
Who?
Who is me? I am me.
How?
How will I find me? By looking.
When?
When will I find me? Now.
Why?
Why must I find me? To be free.

THE HARD WAY IS A GIFT OF JOY It is here that something new comes into our lives. We experience unity, and that means that things once divided and distant are united. Our lives, once fragmented and broken in pieces, come together. Like the knitting of a fractured bone, the broken places of our lives are united and healed.

The way of joy is a feeling way. It is not that the pain leaves and we replace it with joy: rather, the *pain* turns into *joy*. That truth is powerfully illustrated in C. S. Lewis's third Narnian Chronicle, *The Voyage of the Dawn Treader*. This book is the story of a man named Eustace Clarence Scrubb. Even as a child he "loved bossing and bullying," and "though he was a puny little person who couldn't have stood up in a fight, he knew that there are dozens of ways to give people a bad time." From this troubled and unhappy youth, Eustace grew up to be a taunting and pestering man who prided himself on being unsentimental and scientific. He had no friends, nor did he want any.

The degeneration of Eustace went so far that one night he turned into a dragon. At first, he was relieved. Being a monster gave him more power to strike terror in the hearts of those around him. Then he realized that he was alone in the world. Being a monster cut him off from all others. For the first time in his life, Eustace felt his loneliness. He was ready, even eager, to change. But he did not know what to do. The dragon that Eustace had become lifted up its heart and wept.

At this point he met Aslan the Lion, ruler of the land of Narnia. The Lion led him to the center of a mountaintop garden where there was a deep pool of pure water. "Undress," the Lion commanded him. Eustace had to shed the skin of the dragon. He managed to shake off three layers of the rough and wrinkled dragon's hide. But that was only the surface. He knew then that the lion had to help if he were ever to rid himself of the dragon's hide. Eustace later recalled the rest of his experience: "The very first tear he made was so deep that I thought it had gone right to my heart. And when he began pulling the skin off, it hurt worse than anything I've ever felt. The only thing that made me able to bear it was just the pleasure of feeling the stuff come off." Finally, the skin was all off and lay there in the grass, thick and dark and "all knobby." Eustace continued: "And there I was as smooth and soft as a peeled switch. Then he caught hold of me—I was very tender underneath now that I'd no skin on—and he threw me into the water. It smarted like anything, but only for a moment. Then it became perfectly delicious and . . . I found all the pain gone. And then I saw why. I'd been turned into a little boy again."

Being Willing to Be Weird

Not long ago a friend told me that she was going to "cultivate eccentricity." This phrase surprised me because I had never thought of eccentricity as a positive characteristic. To me, it had always connoted being weird, unconventional, or out of step with other people. To be eccentric is to be a character like an old man wearing boxer shorts outside his pants, or a teacher lying on the floor to teach her class. Bag ladies and bums are eccentric. Weird people who do not conform to the everyday standards of our society are eccentric. Us? Never!

I am sure that Moses' mother would not have agreed with my ideas, because she was a woman who did not mind being eccentric. The word *eccentric* comes from two words that mean literally "from the center." The term technically means to be "out of the center or not exactly round." To be eccentric is to be special and rare. It encourages me to risk being different from the rest, and therefore unique, because it calls me to *be who I am*.

M. F. K. Fisher was an author of books on food and eating, who died at age eighty-three. A story she loved to tell illustrates perfectly for me what eccentricity is all about. An eight-year-old daughter of one of her friends had made a newspaper for her family one Christmas. Fisher's favorite picture was a full-page illustration drawn by the little girl: two ovals, one large and one small, nestled gently together in such a way that it was clear they were gazing with love at one another. "That," said the small artist, "is the Virgin and Child." Her mother, thinking the images too abstract, suggested adding faces. The child, however, was satisfied with the picture as she had drawn it and carefully printed the caption "Different people have different ideas of Madonnas, and this is mine."

For me, Thoreau was referring to being off-center when he wrote, "Why should we be in such desperate haste to succeed, and in such desperate enterprises? If a man does not keep pace with his companions, perhaps it is because he hears a different drummer." The truth is that there is a different drummer for each of us. And as Desiderius Erasmus wrote, "It is the chiefest point of happiness that a man is willing to be what he is."

So, let us think of several words that we may apply to ourselves: *special, unique, weird, different, distinctive, exceptional, peculiar, uncommon, unusual, atypical.* We may use these words in such a way as to indicate that we are not okay. If we choose, we may continue to require ourselves to be like everybody else. We may think that because we are not like other people we are less than they are, and condemn ourselves for not living up to their standards.

Or, we may see ourselves as uncommon, irregular, odd, unconventional, deviating from the norm and thus as extraordinary. We are original, and that is precisely what makes us eccentric.

The question we each must answer again and again in life is, How am I off-center, or irregular, or unconventional? That is, what are the things that make me *me?*

To answer that question, we must devote attention to our deepest desires. Please consider the following questions:

1. If you could do whatever you wanted to do in life, what would your vocation be?

   What kind of close, loving relationships would you have?

   How would you worship God (or, how would you express the spiritual or mystical side of you)?

   What would you be or do in life if you could be or do whatever you wanted?

   What keeps you from doing and being the things you have written above?

2. Who is the most unique person you know personally?

What is it about that person that makes her or him
unique?

How, in your opinion, does this person have the
courage to be so unique?

3. What can you do to develop your own courage to
really be the you that you are?

4. Consider the following suggestions made by Alla
Renee Bozarth:
   a) take risks to help others
   and to become your whole self;

   b) be present at every moment;

c) love as fully as life allows and as fully as love allows;

d) accept acceptance.

Amend the Rules

One urgent area of living that we need to consider if we are to find the deep serenity of life is the rules that we follow. Rules serve as guides and determine the direction in which our lives go. They shape our values and become the standards by which we determine how we are doing in life. Moses' mother shook up the rules of the game. Isn't it time we started to forge some new ways of looking at things?

For example, what do you think of the following as a start?

- I will foster exploration.
  I will expose myself to new activities because challenge is important and learning to risk is good. I will remember that as I grow, my interests shift. I will encourage others to risk more, also.
- I will follow my heart.
  I will let the child in me come out and show me what is fun. I will learn to play, and I will play every day. I will keep in mind that laughter and relaxation and fun are what life is all about. I will quit taking myself so seriously, and I will invite others to play also.
- I will avoid excessive rules and structure.
  I will not be afraid to change my mind. Unreasonable organization and rigid programming are out of place for me. I will be a responsible person, and I will plan ahead, but I will remember that nothing

is written in stone. I will feel no guilt if I lose interest in some venture or if I decide something else is more interesting. I will simply change what I am doing and not worry about it. I will allow others to change, also.

- I will make self-esteem a priority.

    I will choose activities that will make me feel good about myself. Every day I will seek ways to do what I enjoy and what I am good at. I will affirm myself and avoid self-defeating statements. I will praise the process, not the result. And I will encourage others to do the same for their self-esteem.

- I will accept imperfection in myself and others without scolding or preaching.

    When I am afraid I will remember that fear is a common emotion for everyone. I will, therefore, reject the notion that something is wrong with me when I am afraid. I believe that courage is being afraid and going on anyway. In all areas of my life I will encourage and support my effort. I will accept myself as I am, knowing that I am in the *process* of growth and that I am not what I will become. I will recommend that others accept their imperfections also.

- I will learn to listen to my own inner voice.

    I can tell what is good for me, what I want, what is hurting me, and what I like and don't like. I will listen to what others say, and consider their suggestions. But I will learn to trust my own inner voice and not let other people tell me what to think, feel, or do. I will encourage others to discover and trust their inner voice.

- I will figure out what I want, not what I don't want.

    I will remember that it is always okay for me to ask for what I want. I won't always get it, but it is always okay to ask. Wishing is good, but asking is faster. I will encourage others to ask for what they want also.

- I will touch, hug, hold, pat, and otherwise physically caress myself as often and as much as I can.

    When, for example, I sit with my legs crossed, I will sometimes gently caress my thigh. I will just sit there and, in an unobtrusive manner, pat myself encouragingly and rub myself affectionately.

- I will find someone, or several someones, whom I can hug every day.

    I will hug with open enthusiasm. But I will never assume that a hug is okay with the other person. I will ask permission first. I will remember that every hug I give gets me one in return. I will keep in mind these words of an unknown poet:

The hug! There's just no doubt about it
We scarcely could survive without it.
A hug delights, and warms, and charms,
It must be why God gave us arms.

Hugs are great for fathers and mothers
Sweet for sisters, swell for brothers,
And chances are some favorite aunts
Love them more than potted plants.

Kittens crave them. Puppies love them.
Heads of state are not above them.
A hug can break the language barrier,
And make the dullest day seem merrier.

No need to fret about the store of 'em
The more you give, the more there are of 'em.
So stretch those arms without delay
And give someone a hug today.

Jeremy W. Hayward published a book in the early 1980s with the grand title *Perceiving Ordinary Magic*. It is a reminder that wonder is all about us in commonplace, and unfortunately unnoticed, events. Life is filled with magic, and little miracles are happening everywhere. We live in an enchanted forest where the supernatural is garbed as the mundane. The earth is mystery, and we must be careful that we do not miss it because we are busy looking the other way.

We find ordinary magic in everyday things. It is especially present in things over which we have no control and that we cannot make happen. Things we control are nice when they occur, but they are *not* magic, because magic cannot be achieved or controlled. Magic happens; it appears. It is unpredictable and comes unbidden and unexpected. It arises quietly and often in a fraction of a second. Then it is gone just as quickly. And it is in that small scrap of time that we perceive it, or else we miss it forever.

Thoreau called occasions of ordinary magic "fabulous realities." He advocated that we identify the shams and delusions that we have misattributed as truth and turn to the realities that surround us. When we "steadily observe" reality, Thoreau counseled, life takes on the wonder and joy of a fairy tale.

What are these fabulous realities of which ordinary magic is made? Here are some of mine:

- I watch the bean seeds I put into the ground only seven days ago quietly breaking through the dark soil toward the warm light.
- I spy a pair of cardinals, husband and wife, in the green leaves of a post oak tree.
- My daughter calls from her home in another state. The happy smile in her voice gives the lie to her words as she tells me, "Dad, my job is from hell."
- I sit quietly in a porch swing, holding my wife's hand.
- I watch a thousand geese flying south in a flowing

V. I can barely hear their happy honking as they make their way to their winter home.

- I witness a hummingbird taking nectar from my Shasta plant.
- I wash dishes.
- My wife writes a Father's Day note for me that says, "When I can picture God as like you, then I can smile and say, 'I love and trust you, Father.' "
- I find myself laughing as I think about something funny that a friend said to me yesterday.
- I feel proud on the day my son buys his first home.
- I feel the warm sweat under my coat during my early-morning walk.
- I see a child peacefully asleep in a parent's arms.
- I see the sun set.
- I hear the wind in the pines.
- I hear a crow call its mate.
- A martin family moves into my birdhouse and stays the summer with me. I know that next spring they will be back. I hope I am.

Ken Macrorie, in his book *Writing to Be Read*, reminds us that most of us go through each day looking for what we saw yesterday. And, not surprisingly, that is what we find. Most of us expect the same, or worse, and we are not frequently disappointed. But what would happen if we started to expect surprise? What if we removed the blinders that allow us to see only more of the negative things we have come to expect in life? What if we started to look for the ordinary magic? Would we be disappointed?

What if we looked for surprises even in those places where life is not pleasant and in those people from whom we expect only the worst? What unexpected things would we see, and how would that change our perception of our own lives and the world in general? Would it make any difference?

What would happen to us if we really fell in love with life? How would our lives change if we really thought, as Thoreau encourages, that reality is *fabulous?* What if we took his advice and "steadily observed reality only"? Would our lives really be like a fairy tale, as he suggests? What if we started to look for the grand things that life would bring us each day? Would we be fools of whom other people take advantage, or would we find that life is exciting, joyful, and wonderful?

We have now reached the end of this book. But we are not at the end; we are, instead, at the beginning. It is as if we have arrived at an open door. Beyond the door is a rich and fertile field filled with the delights of life. Yet it is a crooked path, one that is often rugged and steep. There are twists and turns, and sometimes the way is shrouded in fog and we cannot see clearly where we are going. Worse, we have no road map to show our destination and the shortest way to it. Rather, there is only the invitation to step through the door.

Now is the time to do it, to change the thoughts, habits, and feelings that will open us up to the enormous joy that is waiting deep in our inner being. It is the life for which we were created. Despite our fears to the contrary, we do not lose even the slightest part of our authentic self as we follow this path. We find ourselves and our joy. It is there within us, ready for us. The question is, are we ready for it?

Yes.

Bibliography

Berry, Thomas. *The Dream of the Earth.* San Francisco: Sierra Club Books, 1988.

Bradshaw, John. *Healing the Shame That Binds You.* Deerfield Beach, Fla.: Health Communications, 1988.

Burghardt, Walter. *Seasons That Laugh or Weep: Musings on the Human Journey.* New York: Paulist Press, 1983.

Burns, David D. *Feeling Good: The New Mood Therapy.* New York: Signet, 1980.

Bynner, Witter. *The Way of Life According to Laotzu: An American Version.* New York: Perigee, 1944.

Campbell, Joseph. *The Power of Myth.* New York: Doubleday, 1988.

Caprio, Betsy, and Thomas M. Hedberg. *Coming Home: A Handbook for Exploring the Sanctuary Within.* Mahwah, N.J.: Paulist Press, 1986.

Corry, James M., and Peter Cimbolic. *Drugs: Facts, Alternatives, Decisions.* Belmont, Calif.: Wadsworth, 1985.

Cousins, Norman. *Anatomy of an Illness.* New York: Norton, 1979.

———. *Head First: The Biology of Hope.* New York: Dutton, 1989.

de Mello, Anthony. *The Heart of the Enlightened: A Book of Story Meditation.* New York: Doubleday, 1989.

———. *The Song of the Bird.* Garden City, N.Y.: Image Books, 1984.

Dossey, Larry. *Rediscovering the Soul: A Scientific and Spiritual Search.* New York: Bantam Books, 1989.

Durka, Gloria. *Praying with Julian of Norwich.* Winona, Minn.: Saint Mary's Press, 1989.

Dyer, Wayne. *You'll See It When You Believe It*. New York: Morrow, 1989.

Erdoes, Richard. *Lame Deer—Seeker of Visions*. New York: Simon and Schuster, 1972.

Field, Joanna. *A Life of One's Own*. Los Angeles: Jeremy P. Tarcher, 1981.

Fox, Matthew. *Breakthrough: Meister Eckhart's Creation Spirituality in New Translation*. New York: Doubleday, 1980.

———. *Hildegard of Bingen's Book of Divine Works with Letters and Songs*. Santa Fe: Bear, 1987.

Franck, Frederick. *The Zen of Seeing: Seeing/Drawing as Meditation*. New York: Vintage Books, 1973.

Frankl, Viktor. *Man's Search for Meaning*. Boston: Beacon Press, 1959.

———. *The Unheard Cry for Meaning: Psychotherapy and Humanism*. New York: Washington Square Press, 1979.

Fromm, Erich. *Man for Himself: An Inquiry into the Psychology of Ethics*. Greenwich, Conn.: Fawcett Publications, 1947.

Griebner, David M. "Shadowbound." *Weavings: A Journal of the Christian Spiritual Life* 6, no. 2 (March–April 1991): 31–32.

Hammarskjold, Dag. *Markings*. Translated by Leif Sjoberg and W. H. Auden. New York: Alfred A. Knopf, 1965.

Hayward, Jeremy W. *Perceiving Ordinary Magic: Science and Intuitive Wisdom*. Boulder, Colo.: Shambhala, 1984.

Highwater, Jamake. *The Primal Mind: Vision and Reality in Indian America*. New York: Meridian, 1981.

Hoff, Benjamin. *The Tao of Pooh*. New York: Penguin Books, 1982.

———. *The Te of Piglet*. New York: Dutton, 1992.

Hurley, Judith S., and Richard G. Schaadt. *The Wellness Life-Style*. Guilford, Conn.: Duskin, 1992.

Jones, Alan. *Soul Making: The Desert Way of Spirituality*. San Francisco: Harper and Row, 1985.

Kavanaugh, James. *Laughing Down Lonely Canyons*. Highland Park, Ill.: Steven J. Nash, 1984.

Kidd, Sue Monk. *When the Heart Waits*. San Francisco: Harper and Row, 1991.

Leunig, Michael. *A Common Prayer*. San Francisco: HarperCollins, 1991.

Lewis, C. S. *Surprised by Joy*. New York: Harcourt, Brace, 1955.

————. *The Voyage of the Dawn Treader*. New York: Macmillan, 1952.

Macrorie, Ken. *Writing to Be Read*. Portsmouth, N.H.: Boynton/Cook Publishers, 1984.

Merton, Thomas. *The Way of Chuang Tzu*. New York: New Directions, 1965.

Milne, A. A. *The House at Pooh Corner*. New York: E. P. Dutton, 1928.

Mother Teresa. *Words to Love By. . . .* Notre Dame: Ave Maria Press, 1983.

Neihardt, John G. *Black Elk Speaks*. Lincoln: University of Nebraska Press, 1961.

Puls, Joan. *Every Bush Is Burning: Spirituality for Our Times*. Mystic, Conn: Twenty-third Publications, 1985.

Rilke, Ranier Maria. *Letters to a Young Poet*. Translated by M. D. Herter Norton. New York: Norton, 1934.

Siegel, Bernie. *Peace, Love, and Healing: Bodymind Communication and the Path to Self-Healing*. New York: Harper Perennial, 1989.

Taylor, Henry. *The Horse Show At Midnight and An Afternoon of Pocket Billiards*. Baton Rouge: Louisiana University Press, 1922.

Ward, Benedicta. *The Sayings of the Desert Fathers*. Kalamazoo, Mich: Cistercian.

Wegscheider-Cruse, Sharon. *Another Chance*. Palo Alto, Calif.: Science and Behavior Books, 1981.

Whitfield, Charles. *Healing the Child Within: Discovery and Recovery for Adult Children of Dysfunctional Families*. Deerfield Beach, Fla.: Health Communications, 1987.

Index